A STUDENT'S COMPANION FOR
Joining the Conversation

A STUDENT'S COMPANION FOR

Joining the Conversation

Elizabeth Catanese
Community College of Philadelphia

bedford/st.martin's
Macmillan Learning
Boston | New York

For information, write: Bedford/St. Martin's, 75 Arlington Street, Boston, MA 02116

ISBN 978-1-319-49485-8

INTRODUCTION

A Student's Companion for Joining the Conversation reinforces the most foundational elements in academic writing. While recognizing and respecting your abilities, this supplement breaks down the steps necessary to excel in college writing, build confidence, tackle time management, and write ethically; it provides additional activities to help you draft, revise, and edit college-level work; and it provides sentence guides for academic writing, as well as editing practice. This companion, meant to supplement the coverage in *Joining the Conversation*, gives you additional support for your composition class. For your instructor, it is an ideal solution for accelerated learning programs or co-requisite courses, while the deep integration with *Joining the Conversation* makes it an ideal resource for any instructor who wants students to build a strong foundation in academic writing.

Part 1: Succeeding in College

Part 1 addresses topics that are critical to your success: confidence building, time management, and ethical and responsible writing. This coverage can be a handy reference outside of class.

Part 2: Writing Activities

Part 2 will help you break down writing tasks for each of the Contributing to a Conversation chapters in *Joining the Conversation*.

- Writing to Reflect
- Writing to Inform
- Writing to Analyze
- Writing to Evaluate
- Writing to Solve Problems
- Writing to Convince or Persuade

To successfully complete any writing assignment, you must break down the assignment into a series of steps. Whether these steps are explicitly mapped out or intuitively known, a paper cannot materialize out of thin air. This workbook simplifies writing tasks into manageable steps, with additional useful activities. These activities will help you with the technical aspects of writing, as well as the potential cognitive or emotional hang-ups that can get in the way of the writing process. For example, you are asked to brainstorm, but you are also asked to identify what assignments are asking you to do and to write down what, for you personally, might get in the way of starting an assignment.

I have found that most questions during office hours are along the lines of "How do I start?" or "What exact steps do I follow?" This workbook is, in a sense, office hours in workbook format. For some questions, there is truly no single "right" response, which is why there is no answer key. However, every activity will generate material for you to ponder and discuss.

Part 3: Additional Tools for Practice

Part 3 begins with sentence guides that help you learn to present information and ideas to others, present your own views, and then put the pieces together to write an effective academic essay. If you need additional help, you can also get practice with editing sentences and paragraphs, reviewing the parts of speech, writing correct sentences, managing punctuation, mechanics, and spelling, and more. You can choose the areas where you need to grow, or your instructor can point you to activities based on the specific struggles that emerge in your papers.

The overall goal for this workbook is to help you become an increasingly engaged, professional, and happy writer. Have a wonderful semester!

CONTENTS

13 Activities for Improving Your Writing   93

A STUDENT'S COMPANION FOR

Joining the Conversation

Succeeding in College

Building Your Confidence

Confidence can help drive and shape your experiences as a student, performer, athlete, employee, parent, and the many other roles you play in your life. True confidence is often defined as having a positive and realistic belief about yourself and your talents and traits. *Assertive, optimistic, eager, proud, independent, trustworthy,* and *mature* are some of the many terms associated with someone who has true confidence. Conversely, a lack of confidence can result in a poor performance in those same roles.

Here are just a few reasons to develop confidence:

- **Confidence helps sell who you are.** Knowledge, skills, and experience are necessary and important. If you do not possess and project an air of confidence, others may not realize you have these qualities.
- **Confidence reassures others.** It can create trust in the people in your life, whether they are your peers, classmates, coworkers, or loved ones.

This guide explores the role that confidence plays in everyday success and offers strategies on building your confidence levels around all of the roles you play in your life.

Not Feeling Confident

Have you had any trouble maintaining your confidence since you started college? It may surprise you to learn that you are not the only first-year student who feels this way. Many students who enter college for the first time feel just like you do: not very certain of all that lies ahead and unsure of how to deal with a number of challenges, both in and out of the classroom. Below are just a few steps you can take to help you develop more confidence:

- **Take a strengths inventory.** Make a list of what you're good at.

- **Set measurable, attainable goals.** Ask yourself what you want to accomplish in the next week, month, or year, and then break those goals up into smaller, short-term goals.

- **Take responsibility for your actions.** Make a consistent effort to learn from your experiences (the good and the bad) and own your choices.
- **Dare to take intellectual risks.** Question assumptions, and ask yourself if the things you believe to be true actually are.
- **Examine and acknowledge feelings.** When something bothers you, ask why.
- **Take charge and be persistent.** Remember, luck is 99 percent perseverance.
- **Assert yourself.** When you want something, you've got to ask.
- **Remember, you're not alone.** Identify individuals who exhibit confidence, and make a strong effort to model the types of behavior that make the greatest impression on you.
- **Believe in yourself.**

Identifying Strengths and Setting Goals

Why not start building your confidence by reminding yourself what you are good at? You can start with this simple, yet effective, activity:

Make a list of what you believe are your strongest skills and qualities. Take the time to think deeply and honestly about this exercise before you start. Another way to do this is to ask yourself: "When I feel like I am at my best, what am I doing?" Continue performing those activities to create an increased sense of confidence.

Long-term goals vs. short-term goals: How do they differ? A crucial part of developing, building, and maintaining your confidence is to set long- and short-term goals that you can reach and that are able to meet your needs. Think of long-term goals as the final product and short-term goals as the steps along the way. For example, if you were to write a ten-chapter novel, you'd have ten short-term goals (write a chapter) and one long-term goal (write a novel).

THE CONFIDENCE CHECKLIST

Before examining a series of meaningful steps you can take to build confidence, let's start with the following confidence checklist. How would you respond to the following statements? Be as completely truthful and objective as you can be.

	Yes	No
I believe I know what is best for me.	❏	❏
I feel I am a genuine person.	❏	❏
I am extremely tolerant of others in my life.	❏	❏
I am consistent – I do as I say.	❏	❏
I avoid procrastinating.	❏	❏
I take an active role in classroom discussions.	❏	❏

	Yes	No
I have an inner voice that guides my decisions.	☐	☐
I maintain good eye contact and tone of voice when speaking.	☐	☐
I often doubt myself.	☐	☐
I am able to handle constructive criticism.	☐	☐
I have difficulty trusting others.	☐	☐
I prefer being alone than being with groups of people.	☐	☐
I would describe myself as an outgoing and assertive individual.	☐	☐
I feel I am capable of assessing my true capabilities.	☐	☐
I am an optimistic person by nature.	☐	☐

If you answered "no" to more than half of the statements, your level of confidence is likely not where you want it to be – and you're probably not alone! Keep reading for some proven strategies to boost your confidence.

Now it's your turn.

- Select one goal you would like to achieve in the next month. Be specific about what that goal is.
- Now identify two or three effective actions you will take to obtain this goal. Once again, be specific and include a time frame for performing these actions.
- Think of one possible barrier that might prevent you from reaching this goal.
- Now consider one action you will take to overcome this barrier. Be sure to detail what this action will be.
- Last, predict what you honestly believe will be your degree of success in eventually achieving this goal.

> **TIP**
>
> So how does setting goals help build confidence? Think about it this way: If you set up a series of short-term goals you know you can achieve, aren't you going to feel more confident each time you check off one of those goals? Even better, aren't you going to feel like a rock star by the time you achieve your ultimate long-term goal? There is nothing that builds more confidence than seeing hard work pay off.

Learning from Your Experiences and Choices

Wisdom can often be gained through both good and bad experiences and through the outcomes of the choices we make. If you can accept that you are ultimately the one responsible – not others – for your actions, this is the first important step to practicing this philosophy while in college.

One strategy for maintaining this belief is to not play the blame game; for example, if you received a low grade, be honest with yourself and ask what role you played in earning the grade. Admitting you are the one responsible for your actions and then responding to (and learning from) that outcome will help strengthen your self-esteem and confidence.

Taking Risks

Has anyone ever said, "Nothing ventured, nothing gained" to you? To take a risk can be an unsettling challenge — you can't be sure it will be worth it, you may question whether you have the ability and the desire to attempt something, and you might think about the consequences of that risk if you were unsuccessful.

Now that's the negative approach. What if you turned this around and, instead, took a chance on something daunting? What if you decided that no matter what obstacles got in your way or what doubts crept into your mind, you would continue to pursue whatever you set out to accomplish? Imagine how you will feel when the results turn out to be positive ones.

Another way of thinking about this is "If you remain in your comfort zone you will not go any further." While taking a risk can seem difficult at first, it almost always pays off in the end — especially in the classroom.

Taking Risks in the Classroom

Your instructors have probably urged you to question rather than to simply accept everything you read or hear. If you follow this advice, you'll take risks in the classroom all the time — intellectual risks, otherwise known as critical thinking. You do this when you speak up in class, when you write an essay, and whenever you carefully rethink long-held beliefs.

Speaking Up in Class

The reward for intellectual risk-taking is that you come away with a better understanding of yourself and the world around you. But what if you are terrified of speaking up in class? What if you simply don't know where to start? Below are two case studies to help you start thinking about how to better approach intellectual risks.

Student A read the class material twice and completed all the assignments. They came to class prepared to take notes and was ready and willing to listen to what the instructor had to say on the topic being presented. As an adult student, they were used to participating in meetings at work, and they didn't feel nervous about speaking up, so they didn't think that they needed to prepare any additional material.

Student B also completed the assigned homework and believed they knew the material but also knew they would be reluctant to share their thoughts or respond to questions posed to the class. As a strategy, they wrote down several questions and responses to what they assumed would be a part of the class discussion. When they attended class, they referred to their questions and answers when those areas of discussion came up.

What were some strategies that each student employed that would help them take intellectual risks? Who do you think came to class better prepared? For each case study, what would you recommend the student do differently next time?

Exercise: Questions and Answers

What do you do to prepare for class discussions? Both Student A and Student B are good students. They read the material and did their assignments. Student B, however, uses higher-level thinking questions to help stimulate critical thinking. As you prepare for class, try to use the following generic question stems to ask questions about the material covered. Then take a few minutes to jot down your answers.

What would happen if _____?

What is the difference between _____ and _____?

What are the implications of _____?

Why is _____ important?

What is another way to look at _____?

Examining Emotions

Daniel Goleman, author and creator of the theory of emotional intelligence (EQ), stresses the vital role EQ plays in building self-confidence. One of his key components is Emotional Self-Management, or the ability to make sensible decisions even when your emotions tell you to do otherwise. For example, if you received a failing grade on a quiz, your first impulse might be to get angry. Even worse, you might consider dropping the class. A better strategy would be to take the time to examine why you earned the grade that you did and to allow yourself the time needed to learn how to succeed in the course. Examining your feelings and how you react to certain situations can keep you from giving up too early on something that is challenging.

Exercise: What Makes a Success?

Make a list of the qualities you see in people you think of as confident. Share the list with someone else in your class and discuss which of these qualities have to do with feelings and interactions with other people. How many of these qualities do you see in yourself?

Being Persistent

One of the simplest ways to gain confidence is to be persistent. *Persistence* simply means the ability to stick with something through completion, even if you don't always want to. If a task or challenge seems difficult at times and the outcome may be uncertain, persistence helps you keep at it. Let's look at an example:

Imagine that you are frustrated with the teaching style of one of your instructors. They present the material in a way that doesn't work for you (but it seems to do so for your classmates). You can elect to drop the class early in the semester and perhaps have a different teacher next time, or you could take steps that will allow you to persist in the course, such as working with a tutor, forming a study group, or meeting with your professor for clarification. In the end, you will not have given up, and your outcome could likely be a favorable one.

Ultimately, it is *your* responsibility to take charge of your success and persist — even if you have some setbacks at first. When you feel like you may be about to give up, remind yourself of your long-term goals and how persisting at the current task will help you attain those goals.

 ASSERTIVENESS CHECK-UP

Answer the following questions as honestly as you can:
- Do you express your point of view even when it is not the same as others'?
- Will you actually say "no" to a request made by friends or coworkers that you feel is unreasonable?
- How easily do you accept constructive criticism?
- Are you willing to ask for help?
- Do you make decisions or judgments with confidence?
- How open are you to another person's suggestions or advice?
- When you state your thoughts or feelings, do you do so in a direct and sincere manner?
- Are you likely to cooperate with others to achieve a worthwhile goal?

Being Assertive

One of the best ways to build confidence is to let people know what you want and don't want, how you feel, and when you need help. The more skilled you are at letting people know these things, the more assertive you'll become. The more you *successfully* assert yourself, the more confident you'll become. So, how do you become more assertive? Let's start by assessing where you are right now.

If you answered "yes" to fewer than half of the questions in the "Assertiveness Check-Up" box above, the strategies below can help you feel more confident when you are attempting to be assertive.

- Use facial expressions that are polite and engaged.
- Always maintain good eye contact.
- Watch your tone of voice. Your voice should be firm, audible, and pleasant.
- Be aware of your body language—how you stand, sit, and gesture.
- Actively listen to others so that you can accurately understand what they have said.
- Ask questions when something is unclear to you.
- Take a win-win approach to solving problems: How can what you're asking for benefit both you and the person you're asking?

Developing a Network

When you create a supportive network of individuals, you are being interdependent, and this is a key to fostering self-confidence. By building mutually helpful relationships, you are more likely to achieve your goals and dreams. Here are some strategies for developing this interdependence:

- Actively seek out your school's many resources. This will mean connecting with an academic advisor, signing up for a tutor if you need one, or getting involved with several on- or off-campus activities.
- Foster a valuable relationship with your instructors; ask for their assistance, feedback, and constructive criticism.
- Start a study group by looking for several classmates who are prepared, regularly attend classes, and take an active part in class discussions. Don't overlook a quiet student who may have true insight into the course; they can prove to be an asset. Approach those you've identified and suggest forming the group. If the answer is "yes," decide on your group's mutual goals and the rules your group will follow.
- Coming to college can be a challenging and emotionally stressful experience; fortunately, your school offers counselors who can provide the understanding and skill to help you overcome your issues, so turning to one can be the right thing to do.

Getting Advice from Other Students

The Goal Setter: Liberal Arts Major at the Community College of Rhode Island

Having little idea what they wanted to do upon entering college, the Goal Setter elected to not declare a specific major; instead they chose general education courses to slowly get themself "into the student mindset." High school had been a struggle academically and personally, so a four-year school was not an immediate option. Previously, their only goal was to not leave school early, and now they realized they needed more structure. They connected with an advisor, and they suggested that they first take a self-assessment test and, based on the results, come up with a set of both short- and long-term goals. The advisor explained the value in doing such an exercise and cautioned that they not give up before achieving some or all of those goals. The Goal Setter heeded this advice, earned their associate's degree, and have since transferred to a four-year college, confident that their next goal of a bachelor's degree will be realized.

The Networker: Marketing Major at Bryant University, Rhode Island

Their high school counselor told the Networker that they were "not college material," and they retained that belief until their early thirties, when they decided that they had something to prove to the counselor *and to themself.* They employed interdependence, surrounding themself with students who practiced successful strategies and who regularly encouraged them. The result was a mostly successful first-semester experience. Following this positive outcome, they never looked back, except to wait for the day when they returned to their former high school to display their diploma to their former guidance counselor.

TIPS   FOR CONFIDENCE-BUILDING

Here are some time-tested strategies that will help you throughout your life. By following these steps, you will achieve *realistic and worthwhile* confidence:

- As often as possible, focus on your strong points rather than areas of weakness. In other words, be aware of what is good about you rather than what you are not proud of.

- Make a consistent effort to learn from your experiences – the good and bad (you will undoubtedly have many of both in your life).

- Find the courage to try something new and different, even when it appears too difficult or risky.

- When something bothers or disappoints you, take the time to examine your thoughts. Choose to react calmly and rationally rather than on impulse and your emotions.

- Expect that while some of what you achieve in life may be due to pure luck, a good deal more will likely be the result of your personal persistence and effort.

- Strive to be assertive. This means express how you feel, what you think, the beliefs you hold, and do so directly and sincerely. You have a right to say "no" to requests that are not genuine or reasonable.

- Continue to learn and vary your skills and talents long after you leave college. Embrace the idea that there is no end to learning throughout your life.

- Most important of all, believe in yourself. Identify what distinguishes you from everyone else and what you have to offer. Once you know these qualities, you will begin to cultivate them by applying them in everyday life.

Managing Your Time

You might be the kind of student who thinks it's normal to spend hours making flashcards and outlining your notes in different colored ink. Or maybe you're an adrenaline enthusiast, accustomed to starting a twenty-page term paper the night before it's due.

The problem is both of these approaches carry certain inherent liabilities. Goof off and you'll probably bomb all your courses. Do nothing but hide out in a library carrel for weeks on end and you'll wind up miserable. You'll learn more, get better grades, and have more fun in college if you operate somewhere in the middle.

You've probably heard the Latin expression *carpe diem,* which translates to "seize the day" (as in, make time work for you). Mastering the art of time management is one key to your future success and happiness, but learning to actually make time work for you can be problematic. What can you do to take control of your own time? Read on to find out.

The Case for Time Management

Why bother? We know. Some students don't want to "waste" time on planning and managing their schedules. Instead, they prefer to go with the flow. Unfortunately, the demands of college (not to mention most careers) require serious, intentional strategies. Unless you can afford to hire a personal assistant, your previous slacker habits won't carry you through.

To psych yourself up, think of time management as part of your life skill set. If you're trying to remember all the things you need to get done, it's hard to focus on actually doing the work. Organizing your time well accomplishes three things: First, it optimizes your chances for good results, so you're not flying by the seat of your pants. Second, it enhances your life by saving you from stress and regret. And finally, it reflects what you value—it's all about doing your best.

Need more motivation? Remember that people who learn good time-management techniques in college generally soar in their careers. Think about it: If you're more efficient at your job, you'll be able to accomplish more. That will give you a competitive advantage over your coworkers. Your bosses will learn to depend on you. They'll reward you with interesting projects, promotions, and educational and training opportunities. You'll feel empowered and will fill your workplace with positive vibes. You'll have time for a sizzling social life outside the office. Plus you'll make more money and need less Red Bull.

Taking Charge of Your Time

Freedom can be a dangerous thing. One of the biggest differences between high school and college is that you find yourself with far more independence — and greater responsibility — than you've ever known. If you are continuing your education after a break, you may also be contending with spouse/boss/child obligations, too. But it would be a gigantic mistake to assume that Oprah, rocket scientists, and other type-A folks have some kind of monopoly on organization and focus. You, the ordinary student, can also embrace your inner executive assistant — the one who keeps you on time, on task, and ready for a slice of the action. So, how do you begin?

Setting Goals

Goals help you figure out where to devote the majority of your time. To achieve your goals, you need to do more than just think about them. You need to act! This requires setting some short-term and long-term goals. When determining your long-term goals, it is important to be honest and realistic with yourself. Goals should be challenging, but they should also be attainable. Be sure they align with your abilities, values, and interests. Do you want to go on to further schooling? Have you decided what career you want to pursue? Mulling over these questions can help you start thinking about where you want to be in the next five to ten years. Dreaming up long-term goals can be exciting and fun; however, reaching your goals requires undertaking a number of steps in the short term.

Try to be very specific when determining your short-term goals. For example, if you're committed to becoming an expert in a certain field, you'll want to throw yourself into every class and internship that can help you on your way. A specific goal would be to review your school's course catalog, identify the courses you want to take, and determine when you must take them. An even more specific goal would be to research interesting internship opportunities in your field of study. The good news about goals is that each small step adds up.

Identify one long-term goal and identify three steps you can take to achieve your goal.

Long-Term Goal _____

Steps toward Your Goal

1. _____

2. _____

3. _____

Knowing Your Priorities

To achieve your goals, prioritize your life so that you're steadily working toward them.

- **Start out with a winner's mentality:** Make sure your studies take precedence. Having worked so hard to get to college, you cannot allow other activities to derail your schoolwork. Review your current commitments and prepare to sacrifice a few — for now. Whatever you do, talk to your family, your boss, and your friends about your college workload and goals so that everyone's on the same page. When you have a looming deadline, be firm. Emphasize that no amount of badgering will succeed in getting you to go to the James Bond theme party during finals week.

- **Next, start preparing for your future:** Visit your campus career center and schedule an assessment test to hone your talents and interests. Or, if you know what career you want to pursue, talk with a professional in that field, your guidance counselor, a professor, or an upper-class student in your chosen major to find out what steps you need to take to get the results you want, starting now. What skills and experiences should be on your résumé when you graduate that will make you stand out from the pack? Make a plan, prioritize your goals, and then make a time-management schedule.

- **Balance is key:** If you're realistic, planning for the future you want may demand big sacrifices. Be realistic about the present, too. Always include time in your schedule for people who are important to you and time on your own to recharge.

Embrace the Two-for-One Rule. For every hour you spend in class at college, you should plan to study two hours more outside of class. That's the standard, so keep it in mind when you're planning your schedule. The bottom line is that you simply carry more responsibility for your education in college than you did in high school.

Own Your Class Schedule. Your schedule will impact almost every aspect of your college life. Before you register, think about how to make your schedule work for you.

> **TIP**
>
> **Share your Google or Outlook Calendar.** Keeping an electronic copy of your calendar allows you to share with others at a click of the button. Letting your family, friends, and employer know what is on your plate at any given moment can bridge any misunderstandings that may arise because of your school commitments and may create a more supportive home and work environment.

- **Start with your biorhythms.** Do you study more effectively in the day or in the evening, or a combination of both? Ideally, you should devote your peak hours — when you're most alert and engaged — to schoolwork. Schedule other activities, like laundry, email, exercise, and socializing, for times when it's harder to concentrate.

- **If you live on campus,** you might want to create a schedule that situates you near a dining hall at mealtimes or lets you spend breaks between classes at the library. Feel free to slot breaks for relaxation and catching up with friends. But beware the midday nap: You risk feeling lethargic afterward or, even worse, oversleeping and missing the rest of your classes. If you attend a large college or university, be sure to allow adequate time to get from one class to another.

- **Try to alternate classes with free periods.** Also, seek out instructors who will let you attend lectures at alternate times in case you're absent. If they offer flexibility with due dates for assignments, all the better.

- **If you're a commuter student or carry a heavy workload,** you might be tempted to schedule your classes in blocks without breaks. But before you do this, consider the following:

  - Falling behind in all your classes if you get sick
  - The fatigue factor
  - No last-minute study periods before tests
  - The possibility of having several exams on the same day

CONTROL FACTOR: KNOW WHAT YOU *CAN* AND *CAN'T* CONTROL

When it comes to planning your time between what you can and can't control, it helps to know the difference.

What You *Can* Control

- **Making good choices.** How often do you say, "I don't have time"? Probably a lot. But truth be told, you have a choice when it comes to most of the major commitments in your life. You also control many of the small decisions that keep you focused on your goals: when you wake up, how much sleep you get, what you eat, how much time you spend studying, and whether you get exercise. So be a person with a plan. If you want something enough, you'll make time for it.

- **Doing your part to succeed.** Translation: Go to all your classes; arrive on time; buy all the required textbooks; keep track of your activities; complete every reading and writing assignment on time; take notes in class; and, whenever possible, participate and ask questions.

- **Managing your stress levels.** Organization is the key to tranquility and positive thinking. Manage your time well, and you won't be tormented with thoughts of all the things that need doing. Psychologists have found that free-floating anxiety can turn even your subconscious thoughts into a horror show. Want to avoid unnecessary stress? Plan ahead.

What You *Can't* Control

- **Knowing how much you'll need to study right off the bat.** Depending on the kind of high school you went to (and the types of courses you took there) or if it has been a while since you've had to study, you might be more or less prepared than your college classmates. If your studying or writing skills lag behind, expect to put in a little extra time until you're up to speed.

- **Running into scheduling conflicts.** If you find it hard to get the classes you need, you can seek help from a dean, an academic advisor, or someone in the college counseling center.

- **Needing a job to help pay your way.** Just follow the experts' rule of thumb: If you're taking a full course load, do your best to avoid working more than fifteen hours a week. Any more than that and your academic work could suffer.

Four Time-Wasting Habits to Avoid

1. Procrastinating

Should you have to do assignments that seem incredibly long and boring? Shouldn't you be able to study with family members in the room, even if you can't get any work done with them around? Can't you occasionally blow off the outside reading? Yes, no, and no.

There are lots of reasons why we procrastinate. Maybe you're a perfectionist — in which case, avoiding a task might be easier than having to live up to your own very high expectations (or those of your parents or instructors). Maybe you object to the sheer dullness of an assignment, or you think you can learn the material just as well without doing the work. Maybe you even fear success and know just how to subvert it.

None of these qualify as valid reasons to put off your work. They're just excuses that will get you in trouble. Fortunately, doing tasks you don't like is excellent practice for real life.

Slacker alert: Procrastination is a slippery slope. Make sure you get these tendencies under control early. Otherwise, you could feel overwhelmed in other aspects of your life, too.

EASY TRICKS TO STOP PROCRASTINATION

- **Break big jobs down into smaller chunks.** Spend only a few minutes planning your strategy and then act on it.
- **Reward yourself** for finishing the task, like watching your favorite YouTuber or playing a game with your kids or friends.
- **Find a quiet, comfortable place to work** that doesn't allow for distractions and interruptions. Put your phone on do not disturb. If you study in your room, shut the door.
- **Treat your study time like a serious commitment.** That means no phone calls, email, text messages, or updates to your Instagram story. You can rejoin society later.
- **Consider the consequences if you don't get down to work.** You don't want to let bad habits derail your ability to achieve good results *and* have a life.

---

2. Overextending Yourself

Feeling overextended is a huge source of stress for college students. Why? Well, what constitutes a realistic workload varies significantly from one person to another. Being involved in campus life is fun and important, yet it's crucial not to let your academic work take a backseat.

- **Learn to say no — even if it means letting other people down.** Don't be tempted to compromise your priorities.
- **But don't give up all nonacademic pursuits.** On the contrary, students who work or participate in extracurricular activities often achieve higher

grades than their less-active counterparts partly because of the important role that time management plays in their lives.

- **If you're truly overloaded with commitments and can't see a way out . . .**
You may need to drop a course before the drop deadline. It may seem drastic, but a low grade on your permanent record is even worse. Become familiar with your school's add/drop policy to avoid penalties. If you receive financial aid, keep in mind that in most cases you must be registered for a minimum number of credit hours to be considered a full-time student and maintain your current level of aid. Be sure before you drop!

3. Losing Your Focus

Too many first-year college students lose sight of their goals. Translation: They spend their first term blowing off classes and assignments, then either get expelled, placed on probation, or have to spend years clawing their way back to a decent GPA. So plan your strategy and keep yourself motivated for the long haul.

4. Running Late

Punctuality is a virtue. Rolling in late to class or review sessions shows a lack of respect for both your instructors and your classmates. Arrive early and avoid using your phone in class, texting, doing homework for another class, falling asleep, talking, whispering, or leaving class to feed a parking meter. Part of managing your time is freeing yourself to focus on the present and on other people who inhabit the present with you. Note: Respecting others is a habit that can work wonders in your career and personal life.

> **TIP**
>
> **Social Media Addict?** Online tools like *StayFocused* allow you to block or limit your time on certain websites while you are studying so you can focus on the task at hand. Google "10 Online Tools for Better Attention & Focus" to find a program that works for you.

Two Indispensable Tools to Keep You on Track

Here's the deal. Once you enter college or the working world, you must immediately do the following: Write down everything you need to do; prioritize your tasks; and leave yourself constant reminders. The good news is that a little up-front planning will make your life infinitely easier and more relaxing. For one thing, you'll be less likely to make a mistake. On top of that, you'll free your brain from having to remember all the things you need to get done so you can focus on actually doing the work. Two key items will help you plan to succeed.

A Planner or Calendar

Find out if your college sells a special planner in the campus bookstore with important dates and deadlines already marked. Or, if you prefer to use an online calendar or the one that comes on your computer or phone, that's fine too. As you schedule your time, follow a few basic guidelines.

Pick a timeframe that works best for you. If you want a "big picture" sense of how your schedule plays out, try setting up a calendar for the whole term or for the month. For a more detailed breakdown of what you need to accomplish in the near future, a calendar for the week or even the day may be a better fit. Of course, there's no need to limit yourself—use more than one type of calendar if that works for you.

Enter all of your commitments. Once you've selected your preferred time frame, it's time to record your commitments and other important deadlines. These might include your classes, assignment due dates, work hours, family commitments, and so on. Be specific. For instance, "Read Chapter 8 in history" is preferable to "Study history," which is better than simply "Study." To be even more specific, include meeting times and locations, social events, and study time for each class you're taking. Take advantage of your smartphone and set reminders and alarms to help keep you on top of all your activities and obligations.

Break large assignments like term papers into smaller bits, such as choosing a topic, doing research, creating an outline, learning necessary computer skills, writing a first draft, and so on. And give them deadlines. Estimate how much time each assignment will take you. Then get a jump on it. A good time manager often finishes projects before the actual due dates to allow for emergencies.

Watch out for your toughest weeks during the term. If you find that paper deadlines and test dates fall during the same week or even the same day, you can alleviate some of the stress by finding time to finish some assignments early to free up study and writing time. If there's a major conflict, talk it over with your professor and find a way to work around it. Professors will be more likely to help you if you come to them in advance.

Update your planner/calendar regularly. Enter all due dates as soon as you know them. Be obsessive about this.

Check your planner/calendar every day (at the same time of day if that helps you remember). You'll want to review the current week and the next week, too.

When in doubt, turn to a classmate for advice. A hyper-organized friend can be your biggest ally when it comes to making a game plan.

A To-Do List

The easiest way to remember all the things you need to do is to jot them down in a running to-do list—updating as needed. You can do this on paper or use an online calendar or smartphone to record the day's obligations. Techies love the GTD® ("Getting Things Done"®) system for taking control of tasks and commitments. Google it to learn how it works.

1. **Prioritize.** Rank items on your list in order of importance. Alternately, circle or highlight urgent tasks. Exclamation points and stars—it's all good.

2. **Every time you complete a task, cross it off the list.** (This can be extremely satisfying.)

3. **Move undone items to the top of your next list.** (Less satisfying, but smart and efficient.)

4. **Start a new to-do list every day or once a week.** It shouldn't be just about academics. Slot in errands you need to run, appointments, email messages you need to send, and anything else you need to do that day or week.

Advice from Other Students

Martha Flot
Education Major in Florida

"I learned a long time ago that if I don't start my work early, it's not going to happen. I always open my books right after the kids are off to school and begin with the easiest assignments. I feel really productive and get into the swing of things before tackling the harder stuff. It's kind of like the warm-up before practice."

- **Digitally bolster your memory.** "I keep everything in my smartphone calendar — for me, that's the best way to stay organized. I set reminders for all of my study groups and upcoming assignments. If it's a big exam, I'll set the reminder a week in advance to give myself plenty of time to prepare."

- **Exercise.** "I always try to exercise before I sit down for an exam or a long study session, too. Studies show that exercise boosts your blood circulation, so you can think better and feel more awake. For me, it makes a huge difference."

- **Beware of over-committing.** "I used to be a huge people pleaser. Trying to please everyone and juggling my role as a mother, wife, and student, I learned fast that I couldn't do that and still get all my work done. Once I started prioritizing, my friends and family have been responsive and supportive. It helps having a husband who manages his time well; you grow and learn from it."

EASY WAYS TO MAXIMIZE YOUR TIME

- **Carry work with you.** If you have a lull between classes, use it to review material from the previous class and prepare for the next one. Take advantage of waiting time (on the bus or between appointments) to study. You'll be more likely to remember what you've learned in class if you review or copy your notes as soon as you reasonably can.

- **Discipline yourself with routines.** You might want to get up early to prepare, or set fixed study hours after dinner or on weekend afternoons.

- **Don't multitask.** Even though you might be quite good at it, or think you are, the reality is – and research shows – that you'll be able to do your most effective studying and retain the most information if you concentrate on one task at a time.

- **Study with friends.** You can help each other grasp tricky concepts and memorize important facts and dates.

- **Be flexible.** Disruptions to your plans don't come with ample warning time. Build extra time into your schedule so that unanticipated interruptions don't prevent you from meeting your goals.

John Dietz
Architecture Major in Florida

"My first two years of college forced me to be a morning person. But as an upperclass-man, I have the freedom to pick classes that start in the afternoon, so I've reverted to being nocturnal: I usually study or work in my design studio until 2 or 3 a.m."

- **Go digital.** "I take my computer to all my classes, so I keep a detailed calendar there. My work schedule changes frequently, so I always type that in along with all my assignments."

- **Beware of perfectionism.** "As an architect, you could spend your whole life designing something. Often I really have to tell myself to stop and go on to the next thing."

- **Find a part-time job that offers flexible hours and lets you study.** "I work at the gym on campus, where each shift is just three hours long. They only hire students, so they're very accommodating if I need to change my schedule. Plus, mostly I get to sit at the check-in desk and review my notes."

Carolina Buckler
Business and Political Science Major in Indiana

"Having a double major means a heavier workload, but it's doable in my subjects. My roommate—who's studying engineering and puts in a lot more hours than I do—couldn't have handled a heavier workload because of his major."

- **Start things sooner rather than later.** "That especially helps with group projects because it's hard to find time in everyone's schedule to get together. If you meet early, you can divide up the work."

- **Make sure your employer knows your academic commitments.** "I work twelve to fifteen hours a week as a teacher's assistant in the political science department. The professors will automatically understand if I need to take a study day. Around finals, they give everyone a week off."

- **Socialize at mealtimes.** "My friends and I meet for dinner at 5 p.m. It sounds ridiculously early, but I've found that it makes me less likely to waste time: Instead of trying to start something for an hour or so before dinner, I get back around 6:30 and jump right into homework."

3

Writing Ethically and Responsibly

Thanks to technology, it's easier than ever for students to cheat — so cheaters are sprouting like mushrooms. Thanks to technology, it's also much easier for colleges to catch cheaters. And administrators are cracking down on cheating by making the penalties increasingly harsh.

To complicate matters, there are plenty of students who cheat *without even knowing that they're cheating.* Of course, in a perfect world, they'd get lighter sentences than the people who cheated intentionally. But colleges aren't perfect worlds. They're wonderful institutions of learning that don't like to be taken advantage of.

So let's clear a few things up.

Defining "Cheating"

Cheating comes down to two things: Faking your own work and helping other students fake theirs.

Some of the Most Obvious Forms of Cheating

- Buying an essay from someone else
- Texting answers during an exam
- Sharing the details of a test with students who haven't taken it yet
- Copying someone else's homework
- Peeking at someone else's test paper
- Letting other people cheat off you
- Stealing a test
- Writing answers to the test in crazy small letters on your gum wrappers or on the inside of your bottled water label. (Note: Professors are onto these tricks.)
- Plagiarizing: The most common (but equally problematic) form of cheating

The trouble with plagiarism is that a lot of students don't completely understand what it is. Plagiarism is a fancy word that, according to the *Oxford English Dictionary,* means "taking someone else's work or ideas and passing them off as one's own." Fun fact: The word *plagiarism* comes from the Latin word for *kidnapping.*

It's hard to believe that anybody *really* thinks it's okay to cut and paste whole sentences from the internet into their essays. But given that some people don't think twice about downloading copyrighted music tracks and videos, maybe the concept of "borrowing" isn't as clear as it used to be. What's your stance? Have you ever lifted passages off a website, maybe even changing a couple of words to make it sound more like you? Are you inclined to believe that once something is on the web, it's public domain? If so, please know it's *not* so. The fact remains that copying or paraphrasing anything off the internet (or from any another source) and using it without citing the source is cheating.

Beware: Plagiarizing with intent is one thing. But many college students who plagiarize by accident — they copy quotations into their notes but forget to add quotation marks and later can't tell what's their own writing and what they borrowed from a source — are also guilty of plagiarism simply because they forgot to indicate which parts of an essay are their own and which parts belong to another author. We repeat: Colleges are on a crusade to thwart cheating. If your high school was lax about footnotes or paraphrasing, you need to figure out the rules fast.

The Cheating Problem

In a recent survey of 36,000 high school students by the Josephson Institute of Ethics, 60 percent admitted to cheating on a test during the previous year. Thirty-five percent had cheated on multiple tests. A third of them had committed plagiarism, cutting and pasting from the internet. What's worse, according to studies by Donald L. McCabe at Rutgers University, the number of students who think that copying material from the web is "serious cheating" has plummeted to only 29 percent.

Cheating typically begins during junior high, which is — no surprise — around the same time that grade pressure and academic workloads ramp up. In college, the pressure to get good grades becomes even more intense. Maybe you're trying to get into a competitive graduate program, win a scholarship, or land a high-paying job. Maybe you're involved in a zillion clubs, sports, or volunteer activities. Maybe you have a job and/or kids. Maybe you're taking metaphysics. Whatever it is, you could start to feel overextended. And from there, you might start to justify cheating in your mind. Big mistake.

Why You Shouldn't Cheat

Because it's wrong. Because getting caught could set off a firestorm and totally screw up your future. Because cheating is bad for your self-image and can trigger severe guilt and anxiety.

Because attending college is ultimately about learning new things, challenging yourself, and building your integrity. If you try to scam your way through, you've defeated the whole point of this exercise.

And here's the real drag: Cheating has a nasty way of seeping into other parts of your life, like your career, your finances, and your personal relationships, where it can cause long-term damage. Once you've cheated on a few tests, it might not seem like a big leap for you to start padding your résumé or fudging your taxes.

Why It's Easy to Get Caught

College professors have more time and leeway to investigate their suspicions and better resources to back them up. Programs like Turnitin.com let instructors scan essays and cross-check them against books, newspapers, journals, and student papers, as well as against material that's publicly accessible on the web. Even a tiny, nine-word snippet could give you away.

How *Not* to Cheat: Ten Essential Tips

1. **Avoid friends who pressure you to bend the rules.** Writing a paper is really hard. Doing advanced math and science homework is really hard. Studying for exams is lonely, boring, and *really* hard. But trying to beat the system doesn't pay. Remind yourself of the consequences of cheating. Explain to your friends that you are on a valiant quest for honest effort. Make them watch a lot of movies about Abraham Lincoln. As a last resort, find new friends.

2. **Join a study group.** If you're struggling to get through a daunting course, get together with other students to compare notes and help each other grasp tricky concepts. A study group gives you a support system and a more positive belief in yourself. It teaches you persistence and discipline because the group structure involves meeting promptly at set times for reviews. A study group can also make learning easier and more fun. Other members of the group may have noticed important points from class that you didn't catch. Plus, once you understand the material well, any impulse to cheat will cease to be an issue.

THE PENALTIES FOR CHEATING

Cheating is a much bigger deal in college than it was in high school. Remember, you're not a minor anymore. Once you're over 18 and are caught cheating, you'll be reprimanded as an adult.

- "At minimum, you're looking at an F for the entire course and very likely academic probation or even dismissal," says Dr. Thomas Skouras, a professor at the Community College of Rhode Island. "In most cases now, instructors have to adhere to the school's policy on cheating, so they can't bend the rules even if they want to."

- And it gets scarier than that: If caught cheating, you could end up with a Conviction of Plagiarism on your college transcript. That's the same transcript you'll need to use for graduate school and job applications.

- Plagiarism is different from other student offenses in that it isn't protected under federal confidentiality laws. Think about it: "A student who has stalked someone on campus and has a history of psychiatric illness might not have that information on his transcript," Professor Skouras adds. "A conviction of cheating is much harder to suppress."

Note: How often are convictions of plagiarism overturned? Almost never. Most instructors won't go forward with the charges unless they have substantial evidence to back them up.

3. **Don't procrastinate.** Here's the deal: If you want to write a thorough and honest essay, you need to start early. College papers aren't like movie reviews. You're required to do lots of outside research. Then you have to weed through it all to figure out what's valuable. Next, you have to incorporate the highlights into an outline, a first draft, and ultimately, an original, dazzlingly brilliant work that's all your own. All of that takes time. If you leave things too late, you'll be more tempted to cheat.

> **TIP**
>
> **Make a pledge to successfully pass the course as a team – the honest way.** "I chose to form a group more than a decade ago with three other doctoral candidates, and we followed through on our promise to graduate together," says Prof. Skouras. "It really mattered that we were each rooting for the others to succeed."

4. **Don't muddle your notes.** It's vital that you keep your own writing separate from the material you've gathered from other sources. Why? Because it's surprisingly easy to mistake someone else's words for your own, especially after you get two hours into writing and your brain turns numb. So document everything. Be obsessive about this.

5. **Be a stickler for in-text citations.** It happens all the time: At the end of an essay, a student provides a full listing of all the works they have cited. But in the paper itself, there are no references to be found. "In this case, you're looking at a low C at best," says Prof. Skouras. "Your instructor has no choice but to take off major points since it's impossible to tell the difference between your writing and your references."

> **TIP**
>
> **Respect deadlines.** When you were in high school, your teachers might have negotiated due dates. In college, it's almost impossible to get an extension on an assignment. Your old stalling tactics ("My printer broke/I have the flu/I've been working with NASA on a nuclear laser shield — so can I get that essay to you on Monday?") won't fly.

6. **Familiarize yourself with the proper formatting for a research paper.** MLA and APA style are pretty much standard. If your instructors require a different style, they will let you know. If you need to learn the basic guidelines and rules for citations, check out a handbook or visit the MLA or APA websites. You might also want to speak to a reference librarian. A reference librarian has a graduate degree in gathering research and can be one of your biggest allies in college. Alternately, pay a visit to the writing center on campus or talk to your instructor for advice. Many college libraries offer tutorials in MLA formatting. Getting one early in the semester can give you a big leg up.

> **TIP**
>
> **Flaunt your knowledge.** You must not only list the references you've used to research your topic, but you must also demonstrate that you know where they belong in your narrative.

7. **Be sure to list all of your research sources.** If you're not sure how to list a citation or if you're not sure that your source is valid, don't just put it down and keep your fingers crossed. Talk to your instructor, or ask a reference librarian for help.

8. **Master the art of paraphrasing.** Paraphrasing means restating someone else's ideas or observations in your own words and sentences. You don't have to put the text in quotation marks, but a citation acknowledging the original source is still needed. (See *The Rules of Paraphrasing* below for examples.)

9. **If you need help, seek it early.** This sounds painfully obvious, but it's important to go to the writing center or the librarian *well before your paper is actually due.* Revision takes time and, chances are, your paper will need more than a few tweaks.

10. **If you hand something in and then realize that you used material without giving credit to the source, alert your instructor immediately.** Don't just hope it will slip through. Better to risk half a grade on one essay than your whole college career, right?

The Rules of Paraphrasing

Paraphrasing doesn't mean copying a quote and swapping out a few words. It doesn't mean changing two or three words in a sequence, either. It means rephrasing someone else's quote altogether while retaining its essential meaning. Consider these examples:

- If the quote is "The likelihood of an increase in the growth rate appears dim," you might change it to "The economy improving in the near future is improbable, according to Dr. X, an economist at the University of Y."

- Likewise, "Google has been working to build cars that can drive themselves," could be rewritten as "One of Google's latest projects: a robotic car that takes humans out of the driver's seat."

If you're having trouble paraphrasing something, try this trick: Put away your source material, call up a friend or a family member, and explain the point you're trying to summarize. Chances are you'll come away with something that's clear, concise, and in your own words.

A word of warning: When you paraphrase someone else's opinions or insights, you still have to document the source. The upside? You don't have to frame the passage in quotation marks.

TIP

When copying research material into your notes, write the name of its source and page number directly after it. Likewise, when you copy something from the internet, add a URL in brackets at the end. Use quotation marks around all cited materials. You might also try highlighting your research in a bright color to set it apart from your notes. All of this will make things easier when it's time to make your footnotes.

PART TWO

Writing Activities

4

Writing to Reflect

Writing to reflect is an opportunity for you to present your observations about something. You may be writing about your own experiences and what you learned from them; other times, you may be reflecting on how you reacted to something outside of yourself, such as responding to news reports, pop cultural developments, or new technological advancements. When you're writing to reflect, you are sharing insights with your reader.

Answer the following questions below based on the explanation above:

1. What is writing to reflect?

2. What does it mean to have an insight? How might insights make a piece of writing more interesting for the reader?

Preassignment Questions

Before you begin writing your reflection, think about what you have learned from your instructor and/or your textbook. Next, answer the following questions to get you thinking more about writing to reflect. After writing down your responses, look back at question 5. Ask your instructor, a tutor, or a peer to help you answer any questions you still have.

1. Have you ever written to reflect before? If so, what was it about? Did you enjoy the process? If you have never written to reflect before, you can write about a time when you had a conversation in which you were reflecting about an important incident in your life. Perhaps it was about a moment of triumph, or perhaps it was about a failure or disappointment. What did you say about that moment, and what did you learn from it? How well were you able to convey that lesson to your listener?

2. What are your feelings about writing to reflect? Are you worried about the process? Excited? Explain why you feel the way you do.

3. Being proactive means causing something to happen rather than reacting to it once it does. How can you proactively address anything that might get

in the way of your writing an interesting reflection? For example, if you struggle with procrastination, you might make a schedule for completion. If you struggle with grammar, you might do some exercises in the "Additional Tools and Practice" section of this workbook. If your school has a tutoring or writing center, you might wish to schedule an appointment with a tutor to help you with writing a reflection. Think of a proactive step you can take to write the best reflection you can.

4. What do you want to make sure you remember when completing this assignment?

5. What questions do you have about writing to reflect at this point? Look back at any notes that you may have from your textbook or from your instructor.

Understanding Your Assignment

Fill out this section if your instructor has given you an assignment that involves reflective writing.

Often, your instructor will ask you to choose an assignment in the textbook or will give you a handout that explains the assignment. Your instructor may want you to complete various workbook activities before you are given an assignment. If this is the case, skip this section and come back to it once you have been given your assignment.

Read your assignment carefully before completing the questions. If your instructor gave you a choice of assignments, first select the assignment you are interested in completing.

1. Based on the assignment you were given, what type of writing to reflect are you being asked to write? Some examples include a reflective essay, a literacy narrative, and a memoir.

2. List two features of the type of reflective writing in your assignment.

3. Write any words or concepts you do not understand in the assignment. Also, write their definitions below. Skip this question if all the words and concepts are clear to you.

4. In your own words, in a way that is most understandable to you, retell what your instructor is asking you to do. Put any special requirements, as broad as topic suggestions and as narrow as font-size requirements, in your assignment retelling. Make sure that what you write reflects what you have to do in the assignment by comparing what you wrote to the instructor's assignment several times.

5. If possible, compare your retelling of the assignment with that of another classmate. If your work reveals different understandings of the assignment, please look up words and concepts again together. If you both still have a different understanding, ask your instructor to clarify the assignment.

How to Write a Reflective Essay

Have you ever wanted to share your own ideas, based on your reading, observations, or personal experience, that might be interesting or even instructive to others? That is the purpose of writing a reflective essay. The reflective essay is an opportunity to reflect on or deeply consider what you may have experienced or learned and convey those reflections to your readers so that they come away having learned or felt something new about your subject.

What makes a reflective essay unique? Think about what you have learned in class as well as from your textbook reading before completing the next activities.

Below is a list of steps for writing a reflective essay. You may write ideas under the steps themselves or just skip to the activity under each step. That activity is intended to get you thinking about what to do for each step.

1. Find topics of interest

Activity: Make a list of events that have had a strong emotional effect on you. The event should have happened to you recently, not the distant past. Do not be afraid to make the list long. When you have finished, write a star symbol next to the three most interesting or emotionally powerful events.

2. Narrow the list to one

Activity: For each item in your list, write a brief paragraph in which you describe the event and your emotional reaction. Then, consider which of the three events would be most interesting to others, especially readers who do not know you personally. Choose that as your topic for the reflective essay.

3. Explore your topic more fully

Activity: Brainstorm by writing down everything you can recall about the event. Do not worry about essay structure or constructing sentences and paragraphs. The idea at this stage is to recover as much from your memory of the event as possible. Work on recapturing details that can help bring your reflective essay alive: what people said, how they said it, what they looked like, what clothes they wore, any sounds or smells, or other important details. You may even wish to enlist the help of others who were present to help you refresh your memories. Details make writing come alive.

4. Design your introduction

Activity: Work on an interesting "hook" to capture the interest of the reader. It may be a scene-setter, such as a description of something or someone, or a quotation, or a brief anecdote to set the background. Good writers work to engage their readers right from the very start.

5. Outline the main body of your reflective essay

Activity: Make a rough outline of your essay. You may wish to arrange your reflective essay in chronological order — that is, the order in which events happened. Think also in terms of where in your essay you intend to use which specific details.

6. Plan the take-away

Activity: Ask yourself: What do you want the reader to think or feel by the end of your essay? The answer may involve an attempt to look at something old in a new way, or it may be an appeal to action, or even a prediction for the future. Write down what you want the take-away to be. With that in mind, you can complete your reflection.

7. Revise based on feedback

Activity: Have others, either fellow students, tutors, or your instructor, read a draft of your reflective essay. Do your readers "get" the feelings and ideas that you're attempting to express, or do they become lost, confused, or even bored? Revise your reflective essay based on the feedback you receive from your readers.

How to Write a Literacy Narrative

The literacy narrative is based on your personal journey toward becoming a writer. In other words, you explore key people, books, projects, or other influences that led to your interest in writing. This is an exploration of the connection between you and the world of words—either written or read.

What makes a literacy narrative unique? Think about what you have learned in class as well as your textbook reading before you complete the next activities.

Below is a list of steps for creating a literacy narrative. You might write ideas under the steps themselves or just skip to the activity under each step. That activity is intended to get you thinking about what to do for each step.

1. Explore your past

Activity: Write three lists, each in its own column. Label the first list "Books." Label the second list "People." Label the third list "Other." Then, under the first column labeled "Books," write a list of the books that have been meaningful to you as they relate to your interest in reading and writing. Then, in the second column, write a list of the people (e.g., family members, teachers, friends, librarians) who have had a strong influence on your interest in reading and writing. In the third column, labeled "Other," put down any other influences that led to your interests in reading and writing. They could be trips you took with family or school, movies or other forms of art and entertainment that you viewed or interacted with, special school projects, or any other experience you had that touched your interests in reading and writing.

2. Decide on an area of interest

Activity: From your three columns, choose one item. Then, write a paragraph to yourself about that book, person, or event. Try to incorporate as many details as you can remember.

3. Find a beginning

Activity: Create a timeline. The end point of the timeline could be the present or near-past, in which you have recognized your interest in reading and writing. Then, work your way backward in time, marking key moments going back to the book, person, or event you marked in the previous activity.

4. Outline your narrative

Activity: The organization of the main body of your essay is likely to be in chronological order, or something similar, in a literacy narrative. Create a topic outline, based on your timeline from question 3. A topic outline is a more generalized look at the narrative and will help you to develop the key ideas in your paragraphs and in your narrative as a whole.

5. Flesh out the details

Activity: After you have constructed the outline, you should consider what details to add in at which points in your outline. Pick details that are important to you personally because they will best convey your interest and excitement to the reader.

6. Finish with a bang

Activity: Prepare for your conclusion by writing down the results of your experience in becoming a writer as well as drawing on how that may influence others, such as your readers.

7. Revise based on feedback

Activity: Have others, either fellow students, tutors, or your instructor, read a draft of your literacy narrative. Do your readers "get" the feelings and ideas that you're attempting to express, or do they become lost, confused, or even bored? Revise your literacy narrative based on the feedback you receive from your readers.

How to Write a Memoir

Have you ever had a story to tell? Writing a memoir is an opportunity for you to tell your story. The memoir is a narrative of your life; typically, in shorter works, the memoir will focus on just one event or time in your life that has meaning not only to you but for others—your readers—as well.

What makes a memoir unique? Think about what you have learned in class as well as your textbook reading before you complete the next activities.

Below is a list of steps for creating a memoir. You might write ideas under the steps themselves or just skip to the activity under each step. That activity is intended to get you thinking about what to do for each step.

1. Finding your stories

Activity: Create a Circle of Life by drawing a large circle on a sheet of paper. Then, draw lines through the center of the circle to the edges to create sections, like pieces of a pie. You can create as many sections as you have years in your life, minus the first four or five (most of us cannot remember our earliest years). Then, write *one* key event or moment that happened in each year — perhaps the most important event for that year. Take your time doing this as it may take a while to recall each year separately or to decide which event was the most important that year.

2. Picking the story

Activity: Examine the Circle of Life and draw a star next to the two most interesting events or moments of your life. Then, make a list of the reasons each of those events was important to you and why. Compare the lists and decide upon which event will be the centerpiece of your memoir.

3. Start strong

Activity: Write a paragraph in which you explain to yourself why what you chose for your memoir is important. Think about the event in terms of your personal or emotional development, intellectual or educational progress, or some other change or realization that occurred because of the experience.

4. Outline your story

Activity: Write a rough outline in which you order the events of your life that are relevant to the experience, perhaps both before and after the event. As you look over the outline, determine how much background information must be given about people and events (remember: your reader doesn't know these people or events) and how you can present any necessary information in a coherent and logical fashion.

5. Construct a draft like you're telling the story to a new friend

Activity: When writing the rough draft, keep in mind a sense of the audience. In this case, pretend the audience is someone you've recently become friendly with, and you want to tell that person a story that will reveal something about who you are. The tone of your writing can be lighter and more casual than in other pieces of writing.

6. What is the moral to the story?

Activity: Remember, the memoir conveys a life lesson or an insight for the reader. Therefore, your reader must relate to what has happened. Review your memoir to be sure that the point of what you're saying has come through.

7. Revise based on feedback

Activity: Have others, either fellow students, tutors, or your instructor, read a draft of your memoir. Do your readers "get" the feelings and ideas that you're attempting to express, or do they get lost, confused, or even bored? Revise your memoir based on the feedback you receive from your readers.

5

Writing to Inform

When the purpose of your writing is to share information – about current events, for instance, or the quality of a movie you saw recently – you are writing to inform. You have information and you want your readers to have that information as well. Before you write, there are two key steps you should remember to take:

1. Check your sources and confirm your information. Sharing false information does not help anyone, so be sure that your writing is accurate.

2. Know your audience. Different audiences need different levels of information. The members of the football team do not need to hear the basic rules of the game before you can offer information about new regulations that are being considered by the league. If your audience is broader, however, you might need to provide background so that they understand the information you are sharing with them.

To help you to better understand your audience, answer the questions below. Then, keep your responses in mind as you draft and revise your informative writing.

1. If I had to define my audience in a single sentence, I would say it is: _____
   _____.

2. Three things that are very important to my audience are:

   a. _____

   b. _____

   c. _____

3. My audience is likely to be: (circle the best response)

   a. Receptive to my information

   b. Skeptical of my information

   c. Neutral about my information

Preassignment Questions

Before you begin writing to inform, think about what you have learned from your instructor and/or your textbook. Next, answer the following questions to get you thinking more about writing to inform. After writing down your responses, look back at question 5. Ask your instructor, a tutor, or a peer to help you answer any questions you still have.

1. Have you written a report or other informative writing before? If so, what was it about? Did you enjoy the process? If you have never written a report before, consider a time when you have verbally shared information.

2. What are your feelings about writing to inform? Are you worried about the process? Excited? Explain why you feel the way you do.

3. Being proactive means causing something to happen rather than reacting to it once it has. How can you proactively address anything that might get in the way of you writing an awesome report? For example, if you struggle with procrastination, you might make a schedule for completion. If you struggle with grammar, you might do some exercises in the "Additional Tools for Practice" section of this workbook. Think of a proactive step you can take to write the best report you can.

4. What do you want to make sure you remember when completing this assignment?

5. What questions do you have about informative writing at this point? Look back at any notes from your textbook or from your instructor that you may have.

Understanding Your Assignment

Fill out this section if your instructor has assigned you informational writing.

Oftentimes, your instructor will ask you to choose an assignment in the textbook or will give you a handout that explains the assignment. They may want you to complete various activities before you are given an assignment. If this is the case, skip this section and come back to it once you have been given your assignment.

Read your assignment carefully before completing the questions. If your instructor gave you a choice of assignments, first select the assignment you are interested in completing.

1. Based on the assignment that you were given, what informative genre are you being asked to write? Some examples include: academic research report, profile or news report, and infographic.

2. List two features of the type of informative writing you have been assigned.

3. Write any words or concepts that you do not understand in the assignment. Also write their definitions below. Skip this question if all words and concepts are clear to you.

4. In your own words, in a way that is most understandable to you, retell what your instructor is asking you to do. Put any special requirements, as broad as topic suggestions and as narrow as font-size requirements, in your assignment retelling. Make sure what you write reflects what you have to do in the assignment by comparing what you wrote to the instructor's assignment several times.

5. If possible, compare your retelling of the assignment with that of another classmate. If your work reveals different understandings of the assignment, please look up words and concepts again together. If you both still have a different understanding, ask your instructor to clarify the assignment.

How to Write a Profile or News Report

A profile is a type of information writing that offers a close look at a specific individual, while a news report is writing designed by the news media to provide information on a relevant topic to the general public.

What makes profiles and news reports unique? Think about what you have learned in class as well as from your textbook reading before you complete the next activities.

Below is a list of steps for writing a profile or a news report. You may write ideas under the steps themselves or just skip to the activity under each step. That activity is intended to get you thinking about what to do for each step.

1. Write down several interests

Activity: Write down or draw at least three ways that you spend your time. Do you like to travel? Dance? Play video games? Read biographies? Follow sports?

2. Write down a question you have about one of your interests

Activity: Write down a question that has crossed your mind about any of your interests. Have you ever wondered why Japanese currency contains so many coins? Why the graphics on a video game system you play are so lifelike? Why Lin-Manuel Miranda wrote about Alexander Hamilton?

3. Look up information about your topic on reputable sources online like Biography.com, FedStats, The World Factbook, Data.gov, or Pew Research Center

Activity: Write down five facts about one of your interests in your own words. Please note that the information should be about one of your interests, but it does not have to answer your exact question.

4. Change your research question if needed

Activity: As we research, we often find that there is not enough information to answer the questions that we start with. The truth is there is probably an answer out there, but you may not have time to find it and keep to the due date from your instructor. If your research question is being answered, great. For example, Lin-Manuel Miranda might have been interested in the life of Alexander Hamilton because his father was a political consultant. Reading the Chernow biography of Hamilton certainly influenced him. The fact that he has a son named Sebastian does not seem to answer the question. But perhaps doing a feature story on Lin-Manuel Miranda's family is even more interesting. Let your interests lead the way.

If your topic is not starting to be answered, see if you can write possible questions that come from the information you found about your topic. Try adding the words "who," "what," "where," or "why" in front of a piece of information that you found. For example, you might write, "Why did Miranda use hip hop and R&B in *Hamilton*?"

5. Begin your introduction

Activity: Write about why you became interested in your topic. Switching from our Lin-Manuel Miranda example, you might write about how you have been playing video games all your life and noticed that the graphics kept getting better and better. Discuss the types of games you played and why you are interested in knowing why the graphics are getting more lifelike or why we value this. In your essay, you will write at least three paragraphs for your introduction. But here, since you are brainstorming, just write one. End your paragraph with your research question.

6. Create a rough outline for your body paragraphs

Activity: Write down the type of information you might include in each paragraph to explore the answer to your questions. For example, your first paragraph might be about early video game graphics and early video game audiences. Your second paragraph might be about video game graphics and audiences in the 1990s. Your third paragraph might be about the graphics in a game that you like to play and the audience that plays the game.

7. Write a potential conclusion paragraph

Activity: Write down the conclusions you are drawing from the information you presented. In other words, write down an answer or answers to your research question for your reader.

8. Research to fill gaps and write your first draft, making sure that it is properly formatted

Activity: Identify any research gaps/topics that you still need to look up when writing your profile or news report.

How to Write a Research Report

A research report is an objective (not personal) essay that presents information on a topic that you have investigated.

What makes a research report unique? Think about what you have learned in class as well as your textbook reading before you complete the next activities.

Below is a list of steps for writing a research report. You may write ideas under the steps themselves or just skip to the activity under each step. That activity is intended to get you thinking about what to do for each step.

1. Write down subjects that are personally important to you or subjects you have discussed in class about which you have developed an interest

Activity: Do you donate to no-kill animal shelters? Do you want to see equal pay for women? List three subjects here and highlight or circle the topic that you are interested in writing about. If you have been assigned textbook articles by your instructor, you may want to find a topic inspired by these articles.

2. Narrow your topic

Activity: Let's say you picked equal pay for women. That is a big topic for which you could write many pages. You could do a short report, however, on the recent developments in equal pay legislation efforts across three states.

3. Decide on a pattern of organization

Activity: Circle or highlight the pattern of organization below that best fits with your topic.

Definition – Talk about a particular object by discussing its broader identifications and move to its more narrow identifications. For example, you might define a triptych as a Renaissance painting (and define what a Renaissance painting is), then you might talk about how it was a Northern Renaissance painting (and define Northern Renaissance painting), and then you might talk about how it was completed by the artist Hieronymus Bosch.

Position, Location, or Space – Describe a topic based on where it is located. You might move from the back of the store to the front of the store when writing a report on a crime scene or talk about the periodic table by moving from left to right.

Division – Think of the major parts of a topic. For example, if you were writing a report about how your college works to promote student success, you might talk about this topic first with regard to the college administrative leadership, then the instructors, and then the college's student government.

Classification – Classification is dividing your report into a main topic and its types. For example, you might do a report about poetry and write about lyric poems and narrative poems. You can also create your own system of classification.

Date, Time, Sequence – You can organize a report based on when events happened. You can write a report about a president's significant achievements in foreign relations starting with the first achievement and ending with the last achievement before the president left office.

Magnitude or Order of Importance – This is a strategy that you can use when your material can be ranked. The most acidic fruit, for example, could be spoken about first and then the report could move to the least acidic fruit.

4. Get objective

Activity: When writing a report, it is a good idea to remove yourself, the narrative "I," from your writing. First look up the words subjective and objective in a dictionary, then write why it is a good idea to remain objective in research reports.

5. Write down topic sentences

Activity: A topic sentence in your report contains your subtopic (narrowed area of focus as it relates to your topic). For example, a topic sentence in a report organized by division, about equal pay legislation, would be "California instituted a new equal pay bill in 2017."

6. Find information

Activity: For each of your topic sentences, find one quotation or pieces of supporting evidence that explains what that paragraph will be about.

7. Research to fill gaps and write your first draft, making sure that it is formatted correctly

Activity: Identify any research gaps and topics that you still need to look up when writing your research report.

How to Write an Infographic

An infographic is a report that includes visual elements.

Below is a list of steps for creating an infographic. You may write ideas under the steps themselves or just skip to the activity under each step. That activity is intended to get you thinking about what to do for each step.

1. Do an online image search for infographics or look at an example in your textbook

Activity: What makes an infographic different from another type of report? What are some of the features of the infographic that you found? Is it colorful? Does it have cartoon-like images? Are the images more realistic? How is it laid out on the page?

2. Research information on a topic of interest to you

Activity: Write down some facts. You might look at FedStats, The World Factbook, or SportsStats.com.

3. Draw a picture to represent your topic

Activity: Do not yet worry about representing data/information. If you are interested in nutritional recommendations for athletes, you might draw an athlete or various vegetables.

4. Consider the point of your infographic

Activity: Write down what you are trying to accomplish by creating the infographic. For example, do you want people to know about deaths from gun violence, Second Amendment rights, or youth advocacy about guns. Once you have decided, look up additional data on your topic that relates to your purpose.

5. Draw a draft of your infographic

Activity: See if you can use the symbol(s) that you drew for question 3 to represent data in your infographic.

6. Make a final draft of your infographic

Activity: Make a final draft of your infographic on paper or use a free online infographic-making program.

6

Writing to Analyze

When your goal is to answer a question about a specific topic, you are writing to analyze. To accommodate the variety of questions out there, different genres exist to satisfy the needs of your investigation.

As you construct your analysis, you'll find yourself acting as interpreter to your audience. Your readers will depend on you, the interpreter, to analyze a question and, using the resources available to you, explain the impacts of the answer. Here are some questions to ask yourself while developing your question and analysis:

1. Have I refined my question? If not, how can I narrow the scope of my question to better guide my analysis?

2. What genre best suits the goals of my analysis?

3. Are there any gaps in my interpretation? Have I framed my interpretation in a way that my readers will understand?

Preassignment Questions

Before you begin writing your analysis, think about what you have learned from your instructor and/or your textbook. Next, answer the following questions to get you thinking more about writing analyses. After writing down your responses, look back at question 5. Ask your instructor, a tutor, or a peer to help you answer any questions you still have.

1. Have you ever written an analysis before? If so, what was it about? Did you enjoy the process? If you have never written one, write down a time when you thought the author of an article about a controversial topic didn't know what they were talking about. Was this based on what they were writing about, their writing style, or some combination of both?

2. What are your feelings about writing an analysis? Are you worried about the process? Excited? Explain why you feel the way you do.

3. Being proactive means causing something to happen rather than reacting to it once it has. How can you proactively address anything that might get in the

way of you writing an awesome analysis? For example, if you struggle with procrastination, you might make a schedule for completion. If you struggle with grammar, you might do some exercises in the "Additional Tools and Practice" section of this workbook. Think of a proactive step you can take to write the best proposal you can.

4. What do you want to make sure you remember when completing this assignment?

5. What questions do you have about analyses at this point? Look back at any notes from your textbook or from your instructor that you may have.

Understanding Your Assignment

Fill out this section if your instructor has given you a particular analysis assignment.

Oftentimes, your instructor will ask you to choose an assignment in the textbook or will give you a handout that explains the assignment. Your instructor may want you to complete various workbook activities before you are given an assignment. If this is the case, skip this section and come back to it once you have been given your assignment.

Read your assignment carefully before completing the questions. If your instructor gave you a choice of assignments, first select the assignment you are interested in completing.

1. Based on the assignment you were given, what type of analysis are you being asked to write? Some examples include causal analysis, text analysis, and rhetorical analysis.

2. List two features of the type of analysis you are writing.

3. Write any words or concepts that you do not understand in the assignment. Also write their definitions below. Skip this question if all of the words and concepts are clear to you.

4. In your own words, in a way that is most understandable to you, retell what your instructor is asking you to do. Put any special requirements, as broad as topic suggestions and as narrow as font-size requirements, in your assignment retelling. Make sure what you write reflects what you have to do in the assignment by comparing what you wrote to the instructor's assignment several times.

5. If possible, compare your retelling of the assignment with that of another classmate. If your work reveals different understandings of the assignment, please look up words and concepts again together. If you both still have a different understanding, ask your instructor to clarify the assignment.

How to Write a Causal Analysis

A causal analysis examines factors that produce a specific result or situation and can be written about a variety of topics. Writers compose causal analyses when they want their audiences to address and understand the reasons behind a situation and its consequences.

What makes a causal analysis unique? Think about what you have learned in class as well as from your textbook reading before you complete the next activities.

Below is a list of steps for creating a causal analysis. You may write ideas under the steps themselves or just skip to the activity under each step. That activity is intended to get you thinking about what to do for each step.

1. Decide what to analyze and reprint documents

Activity: Read over any texts that you may be interested in writing about and decide on one or two about which you have a strong opinion. Make a list of features you are going to look for when you reread the texts. Here is a list to get you started.

- Features of the language itself (focus on words used)
- Features of the text (are there headings, quotations)
- Structure of the text (does the text start with a personal story and move to facts later?)

2. Annotate (take notes on) your text

Activity: If you can, get some tools (highlighters, different color markers, pens, and pencils) to annotate (take notes on) what you are going to be writing about. Before you start annotating, make yourself a key here. For example, you might highlight all features of language in blue and all features of the text in yellow.

3. Appeal to logic, emotion, and authority

Activity: Quote at least three moments when the author or authors of the text connect their topics to evidence via appeals to logic, emotion, and authority.

4. Start to make claims about the information you are finding

Activity: Think about any strategies that you think are strong. Think about any that seem weaker. Think about how certain strategies might appeal very well to certain audiences. Think about how much logos, pathos, or ethos the author or authors use and why. Write at least three opinions about why the author or authors made the choices they did.

5. Make an outline

Activity: Organize your ideas and examples in the form of an outline, making sure to structure your argument around your claim.

How to Write a Trend Analysis

A trend analysis gives you a chance to comment on an experience with many types of print and digital works, including novels, poems, plays, essays, speeches, blogs, paintings, videos, and so forth. Writing trend analyses can help you even if you are not cultural studies major because it encourages critical thinking, making you more sensitive to your inner realities and your surroundings.

What makes a trend analysis unique? Think about what you have learned in class as well as your textbook reading before you complete the next activities.

Below is a list of steps for creating a trend analysis. You may write ideas under the steps themselves or just skip to the activity under each step. That activity is intended to get you thinking about what to do for each step.

1. Select a trend to write about

Activity: Write a paragraph about one of the following questions:

a. How has a particular print or digital work/series changed the way people think or act in our society?

b. How has the way people read/view/listen to texts shifted in your community or among you and your peers in your lifetime?

2. List your broad topics

Activity: From your paragraph above, identify and list the general topics that emerged. For example, for many people, podcasts have become a preferred medium for news stories and analysis on popular and niche topics of interest. A sentence about one specific podcast episode wouldn't make sense for this question.

3. Establish supporting details

Activity: Come up with one or two details to support your broad points.

4. Make an outline

Activity: Take the information you've generated in the previous questions and make an outline, making sure to start with defining the cultural shift. Most likely this is the first sentence of your paragraph from question one or a sentence that begins "_____ has changed the way we act in society in the following three ways: _____, _____, and _____." or "Consuming text has shifted in my lifetime in that now it _____."

How to Write a Rhetorical Analysis

A rhetorical analysis is breaking down and commenting on how a piece of writing, speech, or piece of media is constructed, how it achieved its purpose, and how people reacted to it. With rhetorical analyses, you are focused not on what is being said, but how it is being said. You are looking at the strategies of persuasion that the author is using, the language being used, and how the message is constructed.

What makes a rhetorical analysis unique? Think about what you have learned in class as well as your textbook reading before you complete the next activities.

Below is a list of steps for creating a rhetorical analysis. You may write ideas under the steps themselves or just skip to the activity under each step. That activity is intended to get you thinking about what to do for each step.

1. Decide what to analyze and reprint documents

Activity: Read over any texts that you might be interested in writing about and decide on one or two about which you have a strong opinion. Make a list of features you are going to look for when you reread the texts. Here is a list to get you started.

- Feature of the language itself (focus on words used)
- Features of the text (headings, quotations)
- Structure of the text (Does the text start with a personal story and move to facts later?)

2. Annotate your text

Activity: If you can, get some tools (highlighters, different color markers, pens and pencils) to annotate (take notes on) what you are going to be writing about. Before you start annotating, make yourself a key here. For example, you might highlight all features of language in blue and all features of the text in yellow.

3. Appeal to logic, emotion, and authority

Activity: Quote at least three moments when the author or authors of the text connect their topics to evidence via appeals to logic, emotion, and authority.

4. Start to make claims about the information you are finding

Activity: Think about any strategies that you think are strong. Think about any that seem weaker. Think about how certain strategies might appeal very well to certain audiences. Think about how much logos, pathos, or ethos the author or authors use and why. Write at least one opinion about why the author or authors made the choices they did.

5. Make an outline

Activity: Organize your ideas and examples in the form of an outline. Note that a strong central opinion does not have to emerge immediately in your essay.

7

Writing to Evaluate

An evaluation provides your comments and assessments about anything in the world including ideas, people, products, and media. To create a convincing evaluation, you should have criteria for that evaluation. You should also use a writing style that gets people interested in what you have to say. As with many forms of writing, good evidence is crucial in convincing people of your points.

Answer the questions below based on the explanation above:

1. What is an assessment? Write about an assessment you have made in recent times.

2. What is meant by having criteria for an evaluation?

3. Explain why it is a good idea to have evidence in an evaluation essay.

Preassignment Questions

Before you begin writing your argument, think about what you have learned from your instructor and/or your textbook. Next, answer the following questions to get you thinking more about writing evaluations. After completing your responses, look back at question 5 below. Ask your instructor, a tutor, or a peer to help you answer any questions you still have.

1. Have you written an evaluation before? If so, what was it about? Did you enjoy the process? If you have never written an evaluation before, you can write about a verbal evaluation you have given.

2. What are your feelings about writing an evaluation? Are you worried about the process? Excited? Explain why you feel the way you do.

3. Being proactive means causing something to happen rather than reacting to it once it has. How can you proactively address anything that might get in the way of you writing an awesome evaluation? For example, if you struggle with procrastination, you might make a schedule for completion. If you struggle with grammar, you might do some exercises in the "Additional Tools for Practice" section of this workbook. Think of a proactive step you can take to write the best evaluation you can.

4. What do you want to make sure you remember when completing this assignment?

5. What questions do you have about writing an evaluation at this point? Look back at any notes from your textbook or from your instructor that you may have.

Understanding Your Assignment

Fill out this section if your instructor has given you a particular evaluation assignment.

Oftentimes, your instructor will ask you to choose an assignment in the textbook or will give you a handout that explains the assignment. Your instructor may want you to complete various workbook activities before you are given an assignment. If this is the case, skip this section and come back to it once you have been given your assignment.

Read your assignment carefully before completing the questions. If your instructor gave you a choice of assignments, first select the assignment you are interested in completing.

1. Based on the assignment that you were given, what type of evaluation are you being asked to write? Some examples include scholarly articles, web-based articles, media reviews, and progress reports.

2. List two features of the type of evaluation you are writing.

3. Write any words or concepts that you do not understand in the assignment. Also write their definitions below. Skip this question if all of the words and concepts are clear to you.

4. In your own words, in a way that is most understandable to you, retell what your instructor is asking you to do. Put any special requirements, as broad as topic suggestions and as narrow as font-size requirements, in your assignment retelling. Make sure what you write reflects what you have to do in the assignment by comparing what you wrote to the instructor's assignment several times.

5. If possible, compare your retelling of the assignment with that of another classmate. If your work reveals different understandings of the assignment, please look up words and concepts again together. If you both still have a different understanding, ask your instructor to clarify the assignment.

How to Write a Scholarly Article

A scholarly article is a piece of writing that takes stock of something (person, idea, or phenomenon) for readers interested in a particular academic discipline, such as anthropology, genetics, or composition.

What makes a scholarly article unique? Think about what you have learned in class as well as from your textbook reading before you complete the next activities.

Below is a list of steps for creating a scholarly article. You may write ideas under the steps themselves or just skip to the activity under each step. That activity is intended to get you thinking about what to do for each step.

1. Brainstorm topics to assess

Activity: Write a list of possible topics to assess. You could write about how a small town's financial decisions helped their economy to boom. You could assess the progress of a particular medical treatment or a particular political strategy.

2. Find your audience

Activity: Summarize who you are writing for and the type of people they are. What are their disciplinary interests and preoccupations? Are they likely to agree with your evaluation? Explain.

3. Determine benchmarks for assessment

Activity: Write down how you are measuring what is good and what is not. Put a star next to any criteria that your audience may not agree with.

4. Write down evidence

Activity: Write down three pieces of evidence to support your claim. Make sure that your evidence links to your criteria for evaluation. For example, if increased housing values are one of your criteria for economic success in a small town, make sure that you find evidence that the town you are writing about has greater gains in housing values than other, similar small towns.

5. Make an outline for your essay

Activity: Following the format below or one like it, make an outline for your scholarly article.

> Introduction states what you are assessing: (subject and the overall criterion for assessment)
>
> Body Paragraph I: (subject and how it can be measured based on first criterion)
>
> Body Paragraph II: (subject and how it can be measured based on second criterion)
>
> Body Paragraph III: (subject and how it can be measured based on third criterion)
>
> Additional Body Paragraphs: (subject and how it can be measured based on any additional criterion)
>
> Conclusion: (leaves the reader with an important point to think about or tells them what is at stake if topic is assessed differently)

How to Write an Evaluative Article

An evaluative article is a piece of writing, sometimes intended for a magazine or news publication, that makes an evaluation.

What makes an evaluation article unique? Think about what you have learned in class as well as your textbook reading before you complete the next activities.

Below is a list of steps for creating an evaluative article. You may write ideas under the steps themselves or just skip to the activity under each step. The activity is intended to get you thinking about what to do for each step.

1. Find a topic

Activity: Write a list of topics you are interested in, whether they are products you hate or enjoy, social issues, media, or something related to campus life. Then, highlight the topic that writing a paper about would have the highest stakes. For example, if you don't like chips with ridges because of personal preference, writing about a particular new type of chips with ridges may not be productive (or very interesting). If the marketing campaign for a particular brand of chips uses sexist language or seems to make false claims, however, you might have more to write about. Pick the topic that seems most compelling to you.

2. Create topic sentences (first sentences of each paragraph)

Activity: Write down key points in sentence form. For example: _____ is a better choice for elementary school students because it helps them learn.

3. Come up with examples to support your opinions

Activity: Write down one example for each of your topic sentences. For example: Each bag of _____ contains a card that gives information about another country.

4. Make an outline

Activity: Using the information in questions 2 and 3, make an expanded outline for your paper.

How to Write a Media Review

A media review analyzes books, movies, plays, exhibitions, or any other artistic occurrences.

What makes a media review unique? Think about what you have learned in class as well as your textbook reading before you complete the next activities.

Below is a list of steps for creating a media review. You may write ideas under the steps themselves or just skip to the activity under each step. That activity is intended to get you thinking about what to do for each step.

1. Find a topic

Activity: Write a list of books, movies, plays, or exhibits you have seen recently. Highlight the one that you are most interested in writing about.

2. Create a topic sentence

Activity: Write down the points you want to cover in sentence form. For example: The film "Crazy Rich Asians" is the first major Hollywood movie to have an all-Asian lead cast since the early 1990s, leaving a major group meaningfully unrepresented.

3. Come up with examples to support your opinions

Activity: Write down one example for each of your topic sentences. For example: Before "Crazy Rich Asians," the last major Hollywood film to feature an all-Asian lead cast was "The Joy Luck Club," which came out in 1993.

4. Make an outline

Activity: Using the information in questions 2 and 3, make an expanded outline for your paper.

How to Write a Progress Report

A progress report is a piece of writing – often including images or data as well – that makes an assessment of how a particular project or initiative is going.

What makes a progress report unique? Think about what you have learned in class as well as your textbook reading before you complete the next activities.

Below is a list of steps for creating a progress report. You may write ideas under the steps themselves or just skip to the activity under each step. That activity is intended to get you thinking about what to do for each step.

1. Select a topic

Activity: Make a list of initiatives, such as the D.A.R.E program or a campus effort to reduce food waste, that interest you.

2. Determine the criteria for success

Activity: For as many problems as you can from your list above, see if you can determine two or three criteria that would make the program or effort a success. For example, if you wrote about a campus effort to reduce food waste, you might consider whether the measurable quantity of waste has gone down but also how much waste is being compensated for by programs such as recycling and composting.

3. Draw your critique

Activity: Make an outline that proves your point. For the example above, you would make an outline for an essay that explains how the program to reduce campus food waste has succeeded or failed based on the criteria that you determined in step 2.

4. Make a final draft

Activity: Tweak your outline by showing it to a friend to see if they find it convincing or if they have any additional questions that you might not have considered. If your friend thinks of other criteria that should be included, add additional support to your progress report detailing the program's successes or failings based on those criteria.

8

Writing to Solve Problems

Writers who adopt the role of problem solver address problems they encounter through documents such as problem-solving articles and essays, proposals, opinion pieces, and advice. These documents provide your readers with context, the significance of the problem, and one or more solutions to the problem. The idea behind a writing to solve problems is transformation.

Answer the questions below based on the explanation above:

1. What are some types of problem-solving documents?

2. What does the word *allocate* mean? What type of document might involve suggestions for the allocation of funds?

Preassignment Questions

Before you begin writing to solve a problem, think about what you have learned from your instructor and/or your textbook. Next, answer the following questions to get you thinking more about writing a problem-solving document. After responding to the questions below, look back at question 5. Ask your instructor, a tutor, or a peer to help you answer any questions you still have.

1. Have you ever written a problem-solving essay, proposal, or opinion piece? If so, what was it about? Did you enjoy the process? If you have never written any of the above before, start with a problem-solving essay or proposal: You can write about a problem you identified or a proposal you made to someone in your life. Maybe you identified a problem with your city's response to severe weather conditions. Maybe you proposed to a friend that you see the midnight viewing of a newly released movie at your local movie theatre. How did you frame your problem, and what did you say in the proposal? How did it turn out?

2. What are your feelings about writing a proposal? Are you worried about the process? Excited? Explain why you feel the way you do.

3. Being proactive means causing something to happen rather than reacting to it once it has. How can you proactively address anything that might get in the way of you writing an awesome proposal? For example, if you struggle with procrastination, you might make a schedule for completion. If you struggle with grammar, you might do some exercises in the "Additional Tools and Practice" section of this workbook. Think of a proactive step you can take to write the best proposal you can.

4. What do you want to make sure you remember when completing this assignment?

5. What questions do you have about writing to solve problems at this point? Look back at any notes from your textbook or from your instructor that you may have.

Understanding Your Assignment

Fill out this section if your instructor has given you a particular problem-solving assignment.

Oftentimes, your instructor will ask you to choose an assignment in the textbook or will give you a handout that explains the assignment. Your instructor may want you to complete various workbook activities before you are given an assignment. If this is the case, skip this section and come back to it once you have been given your assignment.

Read your assignment carefully before completing the questions. If your instructor gave you a choice of assignments, first select the assignment you are interested in completing.

1. Based on the assignment you were given, what type of problem-solving document are you being asked to write? Some examples include problem-solving essays, proposals, opinion pieces, and advice.

2. List two features of the type of document you are writing.

3. Write any words or concepts that you do not understand in the assignment. Also write their definitions below. Skip this question if all of the words and concepts are clear to you.

4. In your own words, in a way that is most understandable to you, retell what your instructor is asking you to do. Put any special requirements, as broad as topic suggestions or as narrow as font-size requirements, in your assignment retelling. Make sure what you write reflects what you have to do in the assignment by comparing what you wrote to the instructor's assignment several times.

5. If possible, compare your retelling of the assignment with that of another classmate. If your work reveals different understandings of the assignment, please look up words and concepts again together. If you both still have a different understanding, ask your instructor to clarify the assignment.

How to Write a Problem-Solving Essay

Have you ever described a problem you were dealing with (say, paying student loans on time) to a friend who, you assume, understands your struggle? Were you dismayed to realize that your friend just couldn't connect with your problem or relate to your situation? A problem-solving essay seeks to bridge that gap in understanding by outlining and defining the problem, explaining its significance, and proposing ways to solve it.

What makes a problem-solving essay unique? Think about what you have learned in class as well as your textbook reading before you complete the next activities.

Below is a list of steps for drafting a problem-solving essay. You may write ideas under the steps themselves or just skip to the activity under each step. That activity is intended to get you thinking about what to do for each step.

1. Choose a problem to write about

Activity: Write a paragraph about something that frustrates you or about something in your world (school, family, community, and so on) that just doesn't seem right. Mention a few examples and record exactly what about that issue doesn't feel right.

2. Determine those affected

Activity: Consider the issues and examples you recorded in the previous activity. For each example, identify the individuals or groups of people that face negative consequences due to this problem.

3. Find evidence

Activity: Find data about the problem, potentially from reputable media like *the New York Times*, *the Washington Post*, *the Wall Street Journal*, or your preferred local news source.

4. List solutions to the problem

Activity: Once you've come up with a clear definition of the problem and the people impacted by it, jot down some solutions (what you think should be done) to the problem. Looking at previously suggested solutions or solutions to similar problems can help you refine your proposed solutions.

5. Prepare a draft

Activity: Explain the problem using the clear problem definition you've composed. Propose your solutions in your thesis statement, followed by supporting paragraphs that explain your solutions. Be sure to consider and address potential objections to your solution.

How to Write a Proposal

Similar to a problem-solving essay, a proposal seeks to make readers aware of a specific problem and outlines possible solutions. In addition, a proposal can also provide ideas for how to handle a situation and suggestions on the allocation of resources and funds.

What makes a proposal unique? Think about what you have learned in class as well as your from textbook reading before you complete the next activities.

Below is a list of steps for drafting a proposal. You may write ideas under the steps themselves or just skip to the activity under each step. That activity is intended to get you thinking about what to do for each step.

1. Choose a topic to write about

Activity: Record a list of some problems or experiences causing frustration that you can identify. These can be issues you encounter in your daily life or ones you've read about. When you're done, highlight the example that you think a bunch of people are also frustrated about.

2. Define your audience

Activity: When drafting a proposal, it's important to keep your audience in mind. Write down who your main readers will be, including the people who are in a position to change the problem you've identified. Usually these are people with money and/or power.

3. Zoom in on a topic

Activity: Write a paragraph describing the problem you want to center your proposal around.

4. List solutions to the problem

Make a list of solutions to the issue (what you think should be done) and what would be needed for the solution to manifest. When writing these solutions, please keep in mind your target audiences.

5. Find evidence

Activity: Find data to support your proposal. Also find potential objections to it. It will be important to add some objections to your proposal and then prove that the objections do not outweigh the benefits of your proposed solution(s).

6. Make an outline

Activity: Make an outline for your proposal. The most obvious outline would start with a descriptive paragraph about the problem. All subsequent paragraphs (paragraphs that follow) would be about your reasons and the evidence supporting those reasons (usually one reason per paragraph). Consider the best order. There is no rule that says you have to start with the description. You decide how the information you wrote and gathered above should best be organized.

7. Revise based on feedback

Activity: Send a draft of your proposal out for peer review and see what kind of feedback you get in return. Are people outraged? Are they motivated to act? Revise your proposal based on the thoughts and feelings that your audience expresses.

How to Offer Advice

Advice is presented in many types of documents, including advice columns, speeches, essays, and articles. Writers who offer advice identify a problem they believe exists, and they convince the audience that their proposed solution (their advice) is worth looking into. Think about the last time you offered advice to friends or family. What was the specific problem? Were your friends/family members directly impacted by the problem? How did your deliver your advice in a way that kept their interest and convinced them to act upon it?

If you're struggling to narrow down the best way to present your advice, try starting with a simple advice column first.

What makes an advice column unique? Think about what you have learned in class as well as from your textbook reading before you complete the next activities.

Below is a list of steps for drafting an advice column. You may write ideas under the steps themselves or just skip to the activity under each step. That activity is intended to get you thinking about what to do for each step.

1. Choose a topic to write about

Activity: Write a paragraph about what frustrates you or what could be changed in your world (school, family, community, and so on). It helps to consider examples that you have a close connection to, or those that you feel you can discuss confidently. When you are done, highlight the example that you think a bunch of people are also frustrated about.

2. Determine your audiences

Activity: For advice columns, you want to be aware of your audience. Your audience will probably be people who, like you, have a close connection to this problem and are looking for guidance on how to solve it/avoid it from someone who has also experienced it. Write down who your main viewers will be.

3. Narrow in on your topic

Activity: Write a paragraph describing the problem you want to advise on in more detail. Complete this step to make sure the problem you've selected is one that you're familiar with and can advise on with confidence.

4. List solutions to the problem

Make a list of solutions that you can incorporate into your advice column. What do you think should be done about the issue, and what would be needed for the solution to manifest? When writing these solutions, please keep in mind your target audiences.

5. Revise until you get it

Activity: Present your solutions in a way that makes your audience feel confident that you, the writer, know what you're talking about and are offering sound advice. Keep revising until your advice column reflects your knowledge about the problem and your connection to it. Your role as adviser is to convince your audience that you, like them, are also invested in a solution to this problem and can offer solutions that will benefit them.

9

Writing to Convince or Persuade

An argument puts forth your opinion about a topic. When writing an argument, make sure that there are at least some others who feel differently from you. The point of an argument is to help people think in new ways about topics and even create solutions to issues in the world. In order to write a strong argument, you should establish your audience (who you are talking to) and who might disagree with you. You should also make sure that you offer evidence in the form of data, quotations, paraphrases, or summaries from other sources. When writing an argument, consider the strategies you'll use to appeal to your readers – with authority, emotion, principles, character, or logic.

1. Is it possible to write an argument paper that describes the documented events that led to the start of World War II on September 1, 1939? Explain.

2. Is it a good idea to write a persuasive paper for an audience that feels the same way as you? Explain.

3. What is meant by *audience*?

4. What are appeals, such as an appeal to logic?

Preassignment Questions

Before you begin writing your argument, think about what you have learned from your instructor and/or your textbook. Next, answer the following questions to get you thinking more about writing arguments. After completing your responses, look back at question 5 below. Ask your instructor, a tutor, or a peer to help you answer any questions you still have.

1. Have you written an argument before? If so, what was it about? Did you enjoy the process? If you have never written an argument before, you can write about a verbal argument you have had. Remember that an argument in this context is not a fight, but rather an attempt to convince or persuade.

2. What are your feelings about writing an argument? Are you worried about the process? Excited? Explain why you feel the way you do.

3. Being proactive means causing something to happen rather than reacting to it once it has. How can you proactively address anything that might get in the way of you writing an awesome argument? For example, if you struggle with procrastination, you might make a schedule for completion. If you struggle with grammar, you might do some exercises in the "Additional Tools for Practice" section of this workbook. Think of a proactive step you can take to write the best argument you can.

4. What do you want to make sure you remember when completing this assignment?

5. What questions do you have about writing an argument at this point? Look back at any notes from your textbook or your instructor that you may have.

Understanding Your Assignment

Fill out this section if your instructor has given you a particular persuasive writing assignment.

Oftentimes, your instructor will ask you to choose an assignment in the textbook or will give you a handout that explains the assignment. Your instructor may want you to complete various workbook activities before you are given an assignment. If this is the case, skip this section and come back to it once you have been given your assignment.

Read your assignment carefully before completing the questions. If your instructor gave you a choice of assignments, first select which assignment you are interested in completing.

1. Based on the assignment you were given, what type of argument are you being asked to write? Some examples include argument essays and open letters.

2. List two features of the type of argument you are writing.

3. Write any words or concepts that you do not understand in the assignment. Also write their definitions below. Skip this question if all the words and concepts are clear to you.

4. In your own words, in a way that is most understandable to you, retell what your instructor is asking you to do. Put any special requirements, as broad as topic suggestions or as narrow as font-size requirements, in your assignment retelling. Make sure what you write reflects what you have to do in the assignment by comparing what you wrote to the instructor's assignment several times.

5. If possible, compare your retelling of the assignment with that of another classmate. If your work reveals different understandings of the assignment, please look up words and concepts again together. If you both still have a different understanding, ask your instructor to clarify the assignment.

How to Write an Argument Essay

An argument essay is, in a sense, a written debate. You can imagine yourself responding to existing conversations about your topic, agreeing with or refuting your sources as you make your case and trying to anticipate how your audience will respond to your own contribution.

What makes an argument essay unique? Think about what you learned in class as well as from your textbook reading before you complete the next activities.

Below is a list of steps for creating an argument to advance a thesis. You may write ideas under the steps themselves or just skip to the activity under each step. That activity is intended to get you thinking about what to do for each step.

1. Brainstorm ideas about possible topics

Activity: Write down a list of four verbal debates or discussions that you have had in the last year.

2. Complete a focused freewrite

Activity: Keeping in mind the list above as well as any world issues that you care about, write for five minutes about possible topics. When you are done, see if any topic ideas are buried in your freewrite.

3. Consult an online database for topics and information

Activity: Go to an online database at the library (Issues and Controversies, JSTOR, Academic Source Complete, LexisNexus, or others) and write down three topics of interest to you if you do not yet have a topic.

4. Select a topic

Activity: Look over the notes that you have made on the previous questions and write down a possible topic.

5. Narrow your topic

Activity: Write down why your topic interests you. For example, if you are interested in health care, is it because of a particular story you have read or a personal experience? What about that story or experience interests you?

6. Make a thesis statement

Activity: Turn your topic into a potential thesis statement by writing a claim about it. Your claim is your opinion. For example, even with good health insurance, dealing with the paperwork and red tape of getting coverage for your care during a health crisis contributes unnecessary stress and uncertainty to the situation. Health insurance companies should streamline their processes, accepting doctor recommendations for care rather than challenging their necessity.

7. Determine the assumption behind your claim

Activity: To be the most sensitive writer possible to your audience, think about the assumption that is underneath your claim. Consider the claim "Health insurance companies should streamline their processes, accepting doctor recommendations for care rather than challenging their necessity." One assumption of this claim is that the doctor would only recommend care that is necessary. Some audiences may not agree with this, so you would need to try to get your audience on board with your assumption as well as with your claim. Write your assumption or assumptions here.

8. Write at least one counterargument for your claim

Activity: Write down why people may not agree with you so that you can incorporate this into your essay and get those people on board. Some people like to write the counterargument in their first paragraph, even before their thesis statement, to bring the other side in right away. Others like to wait to talk about counterarguments in individual paragraphs. For now, list at least three reasons why someone may not agree with your thesis.

9. Write down supporting details

Activity: Write down at least four details to support your claim. They may be as broad or as focused as you like.

10. Find data

Activity: Using a library database (Issues and Controversies, JSTOR, Academic Source Complete, LexisNexus, or others), find at least four examples, statistics, or numbers that support your point, and write down at least three of them.

11. Find quotations

Activity: Write one or two lines from an article in quotation marks with the proper citation. Quotation marks look like this: " ". Note: When finding a quotation from an article, you should not look for what is already in quotation marks in that article. You can quote any line or lines from that article in your own writing. When you put quotation marks around it, you are showing that it comes from a source other than yourself.

12. Make appeals

Activity: Write down one or two appeals for your argument that fit into each of the following categories: an appeal to emotion; an appeal to principles, values, and beliefs; an appeal to character; and an appeal to logic.

13. Make topic sentences for body paragraphs

Activity: Using the information above, make topic sentences for your body paragraphs. Topic sentences are always general, which means they are signposts for what is to come in that paragraph. They usually contain a restatement of the claim and the example you are going to talk about in that paragraph. An example of a topic sentence is as follows: Insurance companies should handle any necessary background checks or evaluations before deciding to cover a particular doctor under their plan, so that any medical care prescribed by a covered doctor is automatically covered under the insurance.

14. Think of an order for presenting information

Activity: Write down which of your topic sentences is the most convincing. Why do you think it will convince readers the most? This will help you decide on an order for your information when writing your outline.

15. Think about your outline

Activity: Write down what, if anything, your instructor said about the process of making an outline. If your instructor did not yet say anything, write down what you already know about writing outlines. Many instructors differ in their opinions about writing outlines. Some instructors will give you a structure for writing your essay, and others will want that structure to come entirely from you. Which do you think your instructor prefers? Which do you prefer?

16. Write an outline

Activity: Make an outline using the information you have. Here is one structure for an outline:

> Introduction: (counterarguments and thesis statement)
>
> Body Paragraph I: (least convincing topic sentence and supporting evidence)
>
> Body Paragraph II: (more convincing topic sentence and supporting evidence)
>
> Additional Body Paragraphs: (increasingly convincing topic sentences and supporting evidence, ending with the most convincing topic sentence and evidence)
>
> Conclusion: (summary of argument with memorable final thought)

How to Write an Open Letter

An open letter is an argument or persuasive statement that is explicitly made to more than one audience: the person or organization to whom it is addressed and the general public.

What makes an open letter unique? Think about what you learned in class as well as your from textbook reading before you complete the next activities.

Below is a list of steps for creating an open letter. You may write ideas under the steps themselves or just skip to the activity under each step. That activity is intended to get you thinking about what to do for each step.

1. Consider companies or public figures who have made decisions you would like to address.

Activity: Remember that an open letter is not just intended for the recipient, but for the general public as well. Because of this, you will want to address your letter to an organization or to a public figure of some sort. Consider your letter as a response to a decision or action made by that organization or individual.

2. Write the action you are addressing.

Activity: What decision or action did the organization or individual make that prompted your letter? Why do you feel the need to respond? What action would you like to see in response to your letter?

3. Write down the key points in the decision or action that you would like to address

Activity: Make a list of the key points or elements that you want to address in your open letter. Are there any specific quotes you should respond to? Are there images or video that you should reference or include? If you are addressing an action, what are the implications of that action that need to be considered by the audience for your letter?

4. Make an outline for your letter

Activity: Using the outline below as a model (if you would like to use a model), make an outline for your refutation argument.

Introduction (clear statement of the primary audience and the decision or action that you would like to address)

Body Paragraph I (discussion of specific key point or implication and why this action ties into your overall concern)

Body Paragraph II (discussion of a second specific key point or implication and why this action ties into your overall concern)

Additional Body Paragraphs (discussion of third or additional specific key points or implications and why these actions tie into your overall concern)

Conclusion (direct statement of your stance on the topic as well as any requests for action on the part of the audience)

PART THREE

Additional Tools for Practice

10

Sentence Guides for Academic Writers

Being a college student means being a college writer. No matter what field you are studying, your instructors will ask you to make sense of what you are learning through writing. When you work on writing assignments in college, you are, in most cases, being asked to write for an academic audience.

Writing academically means thinking academically – asking a lot of questions, digging into the ideas of others, and entering into scholarly debates and academic conversations. As a college writer, you will be asked to read different kinds of texts; understand and evaluate authors' ideas, arguments, and methods; and contribute your own ideas. In this way, you present yourself as a participant in an academic conversation.

What does it mean to be part of an *academic conversation*? Well, think of it this way: You and your friends may have an ongoing debate about the best film trilogy of all time. During your conversations with one another, you analyze the details of the films, introduce points you want your friends to consider, listen to their ideas, and perhaps cite what the critics have said about a particular trilogy. This kind of conversation is not unlike what happens among scholars in academic writing – except they could be debating the best public policy for a social problem or the most promising new theory in treating disease.

If you are uncertain about what academic writing *sounds like* or if you're not sure you're any good at it, this chapter offers guidance for you at the sentence level. It helps answer questions such as these:

How can I present the ideas of others in a way that demonstrates my understanding of the debate?

How can I agree with someone, but add a new idea?

How can I disagree with a scholar without seeming, well, rude?

How can I make clear in my writing which ideas are mine and which ideas are someone else's?

The following sections offer sentence guides for you to use and adapt to your own writing situations. As in all writing that you do, you will have to think about your purpose (reason for writing) and your audience (readers) before knowing which guides will be most appropriate for a particular piece of writing or for a certain part of your essay.

The guides are organized to help you present background information, the views and claims of others, and your own views and claims—all in the context of your purpose and audience.

Academic Writers Present Information and Others' Views

When you write in academic situations, you may be asked to spend some time giving background information for or setting a context for your main idea or argument. This often requires you to present or summarize what is known or what has already been said in relation to the question you are asking in your writing.

Presenting What Is Known or Assumed

When you write, you will find that you occasionally need to present something that is known, such as a specific fact or a statistic. The following structures are useful when you are providing background information.

➤ As we know from history, _____.

➤ X has shown that _____.

➤ Research by X and Y suggests that _____.

➤ According to X, _____ percent
   of are/favor _____.

In other situations, you may have the need to present information that is assumed or that is conventional wisdom.

➤ People often believe that _____.

➤ Conventional wisdom leads us to believe _____.

➤ Many Americans share the idea that _____.

➤ _____ is a widely held belief.

In order to challenge an assumption or a widely held belief, you have to acknowledge it first. Doing so lets your readers believe that you are placing your ideas in an appropriate context.

➤ Although many people are led to believe X, there is significant benefit to considering the merits of Y.

➤ College students tend to believe that _____ when, in fact, the opposite is much more likely to be the case.

Presenting Others' Views

As a writer, you build your own *ethos,* or credibility, by being able to fairly and accurately represent the views of others. As an academic writer, you will be expected to demonstrate your understanding of a text by summarizing the views or arguments of its author(s). To do so, you may use language such as the following:

➤ X argues that _____.

➤ X emphasizes the need for _____.

➤ In this important article, X and Y claim _____
    _____.

➤ X endorses _____ because _____.

➤ X and Y have recently criticized the idea that _____.

➤ _____, according to X, is the most critical cause of _____.

Although you will create your own variations of these sentences as you draft and revise, the guides can be useful tools for thinking through how best to present another writer's claim or finding clearly and concisely.

Presenting Direct Quotations

When the exact words of a source are important for accuracy, authority, emphasis, or flavor, you will want to use a direct quotation. Ordinarily, you will present direct quotations with language of your own that suggests how you are using the source.

➤ X characterizes the problem this way: " . . . "

➤ According to X, _____ is defined as " . . . "

➤ " . . . ," explains X.

➤ X argues strongly in favor of the policy, pointing out that " . . . "

NOTE: You will generally cite direct quotations according to the documentation style your readers expect. MLA style, often used in English and in other humanities courses, recommends using the author name paired with a page number, if there is one. APA style, used in most social sciences, requires the year of publication generally after the mention of the source, with page numbers after the quoted material. In *Chicago* style, used in history and in some humanities courses, writers use superscript numbers (like this[6]) to refer readers to footnotes or endnotes. In-text citations, like the ones shown below, refer readers to entries in the works cited or reference list.

MLA   Lazarín argues that our overreliance on testing in K-12 schools "does not put students first" (20).

APA   Lazarín (2014) argues that our overreliance on testing in K-12 schools "does not put students first." (p. 20)

Chicago   Lazarín argues that our overreliance on testing in K-12 schools "does not put students first."[6]

Many writers use direct quotations to advance an argument of their own:

> Standardized testing makes it easier for administrators to measure student

Student writer's idea   performance, but it may not be the best way to measure it. Too much testing wears students out and communicates the idea that recall is the most important skill we

Source's idea   want them to develop. Even education policy advisor Melissa Lazarín argues that our overreliance on testing in K-12 schools "does not put students first" (20).

Presenting Alternative Views

Most debates, whether they are scholarly or popular, are complex – often with more than two sides to an issue. Sometimes you will have to synthesize the views of multiple participants in the debate before you introduce your own ideas.

➤ On the one hand, X reports that _____, but on the other hand, Y insists that _____ .

➤ Even though X endorses the policy, Y refers to it as " . . . "

➤ X, however, isn't convinced and instead argues _____ .

➤ X and Y have supported the theory in the past, but new research by Z suggests that _____ .

Academic Writers Present Their Own Views

When you write for an academic audience, you will indeed have to demonstrate that you are familiar with the views of others who are asking the same kinds of questions as you are. Much writing that is done for academic purposes asks you to put your arguments in the context of existing arguments – in a way asking you to connect the known to the new. When you are asked to write a summary or an informative text, your own views and arguments are generally not called for. However, much of the writing you will be assigned to do in college asks you to take a persuasive stance and present a reasoned argument – at times in response to a single text and, at other times, in response to multiple texts.

Presenting Your Own Views: Agreement and Extension

Sometimes you agree with the author of a source.

➤ X's argument is convincing because _____ .

➤ Because X's approach is so _____, it is the best way

    to _____ .

➤ X makes an important point when she says _____ .

Other times you find you agree with the author of a source, but you want to extend the point or go a bit deeper in your own investigation. In a way, you acknowledge the source for getting you so far in the conversation, but then you move the conversation along with a related comment or finding.

➤ X's proposal for _____ is indeed worth

    considering. Going one step further, _____ .

➤ X makes the claim that _____ . By extension, isn't it

    also true, then, that _____ ?

➤ _____ has been adequately explained by X. Now,

    let's move beyond that idea and ask whether _____ .

Presenting Your Own Views: Queries and Skepticism

You may be intimidated when you're asked to talk back to a source, especially if the source is a well-known scholar or expert or even just a frequent voice in a particular debate. College-level writing asks you to be skeptical, however, and approach academic questions with the mind of an investigator. It is acceptable to doubt, to question, to challenge – as the result is often new knowledge or understanding about a subject.

➤ Couldn't it also be argued that _____ ?

➤ But is everyone willing to agree that this is the case?

➤ While X insists that _____ is so, he is

    perhaps asking the wrong question to begin with.

➤ The claims that X and Y have made, while intelligent and well meaning, leave

    many unconvinced because they have failed to consider _____ .

Presenting Your Own Views: Disagreement or Correction

You may find that at times the only response you have to a text or to an author is complete disagreement.

➤ X's claims about _____ are completely misguided.

➤ X presents a long metaphor comparing _____ to _____ ;

    in the end, the comparison is unconvincing because _____ .

A NOTE ABOUT USING THE FIRST PERSON ("I")

Some disciplines look favorably upon the use of the first person "I" in academic writing. Others do not and instead stick to using third person. If you are given a writing assignment for a class, you are better off asking what your instructor prefers or reading through any samples given than *guessing* what might be expected.

First person (I, me, my, we, us, our)

> I question Heddinger's methods and small sample size.

> Harnessing children's technology obsession in the classroom is, I believe, the key to improving learning.

> Lanza's interpretation focuses on circle imagery as symbolic of the family; my analysis leads me in a different direction entirely.

> We would, in fact, benefit from looser laws about farming on our personal property.

Third person (names and other nouns)

> Heddinger's methods and small sample size are questionable.

> Harnessing children's technology obsession in the classroom is the key to improving learning.

> Lanza's interpretation focuses on circle imagery as symbolic of the family; other readers' analyses may point in a different direction entirely.

> Many Americans would, in fact, benefit from looser laws about farming on personal property.

You may feel that not being able to use "I" in an essay in which you present your ideas about a topic is unfair or will lead to weaker statements. Know that you can make a strong argument even if you write in the third person.

It can be tempting to disregard a source completely if you detect a piece of information that strikes you as false or that you know to be untrue.

➤ Although X reports that _____, recent studies indicate that is not the case.

➤ While X and Y insist that _____ is so, an examination of their figures shows that they have made an important miscalculation.

Presenting and Countering Objections to Your Argument

Effective college writers know that their arguments are stronger when they can anticipate objections that others might make.

➤ Some will object to this proposal on the grounds that _____.

➤ Not everyone will embrace _____; they may argue instead that _____.

Countering, or responding to, opposing voices fairly and respectfully strengthens your writing and your *ethos,* or credibility.

➤ X and Y might contend that this interpretation is faulty; however, _____.

➤ Most _____ believe that there is too much risk in this approach. But what they have failed to take into consideration is _____.

Academic Writers Persuade by Putting It All Together

Readers of academic writing often want to know what's at stake in a particular debate or text. They want to know why it is that they should care and that they should keep reading. Aside from crafting individual sentences, you must, of course, keep the bigger picture in mind as you attempt to persuade, inform, evaluate, or review.

Presenting Stakeholders

When you write, you may be doing so as a member of a group affected by the research conversation you have entered. For example, you may be among the thousands of students in your state whose level of debt may change as a result of new laws about financing a college education. In this case, you are a *stakeholder* in the matter. In other words, you have an interest in the matter as a person who could be impacted by the outcome of a decision. On the other hand, you may be writing as an investigator of a topic that interests you but that you aren't directly connected with. You may be persuading your audience on behalf of a group of interested stakeholders – a group of which you yourself are not a member.

You can give your writing some teeth if you make it clear who is being affected by the discussion of the issue and the decisions that have been or will be made about the issue. The groups of stakeholders are highlighted in the following sentences:

➤ Viewers of Kurosawa's films may not agree with X that _____.

➤ The research will come as a surprise to parents of children with Type 1 diabetes.

➤ X's claims have the power to offend potentially every low-wage earner in the state.

➤ Marathoners might want to reconsider their training regimen if stories such as those told by X and Y are validated by the medical community.

Presenting the "So What"

For readers to be motivated to read your writing, they have to feel as if you're addressing something that matters to them, addressing something that matters very much to you, or addressing something that should matter to us all. Good academic writing often hooks readers with a sense of urgency – a serious response to a reader's "So what?"

➤ Having a frank discussion about _____ now will put us in a far better position to deal with _____ in the future. If we are unwilling or unable to do so, we risk _____ .

➤ Such a breakthrough will affect _____ in three significant ways.

➤ It is easy to believe that the stakes aren't high enough to be alarming; in fact, _____ will be affected by _____ .

➤ Widespread disapproval of and censorship of such fiction/films/art will mean _____ for us in the future. Culture should represent _____ .

➤ _____ could bring about unprecedented opportunities for _____ to participate in _____ , something never seen before.

➤ New experimentation in _____ could allow scientists to investigate _____ in ways they couldn't have imagined _____ years ago.

Presenting the Players and Positions in a Debate

Some disciplines ask writers to compose a review of the literature as a part of a larger project—or sometimes as a freestanding assignment. In a review of the literature, the writer sets forth a research question, summarizes the key sources that have addressed the question, puts the current research in the context of other voices in the research conversation, and identifies any gaps in the research.

Writing that presents a debate, its players, and their positions can often be lengthy. What follows, however, can give you the sense of the flow of ideas and turns in such a piece of writing.

Student writer states the problem.

_____ affects more than 30% of children in America, and signs point to a worsening situation in years to come because of A, B, and C. Solutions to the problem have eluded even the sharpest policy minds and brightest researchers.

Student writer summarizes the views of others on the topic.

In an important 2003 study, W found that _____, which pointed to more problems than solutions. [. . .] Research by X and Y made strides in our understanding of _____ but still didn't offer specific strategies for children and families struggling to _____. [. . .] When Z rejected both the methods and the findings of X and Y, arguing that

Student writer presents their view in the context of current research.

_____, policymakers and health-care experts were optimistic. [. . .] *Too much discussion of _____, however, and too little discussion of _____, may lead us to solutions that are ultimately too expensive to sustain.*

Using Appropriate Signal Verbs

Verbs matter. Using a variety of verbs in your sentences can add strength and clarity as you present others' views and your own views.

WHEN YOU WANT TO PRESENT A VIEW FAIRLY NEUTRALLY

acknowledges	observes
adds	points out
admits	reports
comments	suggests
contends	writes
notes	

➤ X points out that the plan had unintended outcomes.

WHEN YOU WANT TO PRESENT A STRONGER VIEW

argues	emphasizes
asserts	insists
declares	

➤ Y argues in favor of a ban on _____; but Z insists the plan is misguided.

WHEN YOU WANT TO SHOW AGREEMENT

agree
confirms
endorses

➤ An endorsement of X's position is smart for a number of reasons.

WHEN YOU WANT TO SHOW CONTRAST OR DISAGREEMENT

compares	refutes
denies	rejects
disputes	

➤ The town must come together and reject X's claims that _____ is in the best interest of the citizens.

WHEN YOU WANT TO ANTICIPATE AN OBJECTION

admits
acknowledges
concedes

➤ Y admits that closer study of _____, with a much larger sample size, is necessary for _____ .

11

Writing Grammatically Correct Sentences

Correcting Sentence Boundary Issues

Sometimes we need to set personal boundaries in life. Have you ever been in a relationship where a friend or a person you are dating only wants to spend time with you and maybe even acts like you are one and the same person? Depending on your personality and needs, you might have brought the issue to the person's attention and said that you needed space to be your own person. This means you set a personal boundary. Sentences need boundaries too. They need to be complete on their own, and they need appropriate space from other sentences to communicate their full meaning.

What is often tricky about sentence boundaries is that they are based in grammatical rules and not whatever you might think is logical. If you haven't spent a lot of time reading books, articles, and other print materials and observing how sentences function in them, you will need to learn how sentences function grammatically to understand their boundaries and how to write them with confidence. Do not despair! In the age of social media, there is mass confusion about what makes up a complete sentence, and many would argue that the rules will eventually change to meet our evolving needs. For now, here are some activities to help you learn how to set sentence boundaries correctly.

Activities

Take a look at the sentences below and circle which is correct:

1. I often go to parties with my friends, my friends are more social than I am.

2. I often go to parties with my friends; my friends are more social than I am.

3. I often go to parties with my friends, but my friends are more social than I am.

The final sentence might be the best option, but both of the last two sentences are grammatically correct. Some students think that the first is correct because the topic stays the same throughout the sentence. You are writing about friends and parties the whole time, so that should be a complete sentence, right? In other languages, such as Japanese, sentences are arranged by topic, but this is not true in English. The first sentence is a type of run-on sentence called a comma splice. It is missing the appropriate punctuation, instead splicing together two complete thoughts with only a comma. These two complete thoughts need better boundaries than what a comma provides.

In order to have a complete sentence, you need to have at least one complete thought, at least one verb, and at least one subject. Grammatically speaking, a "complete thought" is what we call an **independent clause**. It's independent because, much like an independent person with good boundaries, it is complete and can stand alone. "I often go to parties with my friends" is an independent clause because it has a subject ("I"), a verb ("go"), and is a complete thought that can stand alone as its own complete sentence. Likewise, "My friends are more social than I am" is also an independent clause because it has a subject ("My friends"), a verb ("are"), and is a complete thought that can stand alone as its own complete sentence as well.

If you have two separate independent clauses and they are fused together (meaning, no punctuation divides them) or spliced together with a comma (as in example 1), they form a **run-on sentence**, which means they have poor boundaries and are grammatically incorrect.

To put two or more independent clauses into a single complete sentence requires the use of either a **conjunction** (such as *and, but, for, or,* or *so*) preceded by a comma (example 3) or a stronger linking punctuation mark than a comma (such as a colon or a semicolon, as in example 2). When two independent clauses are properly joined, as in examples 2 and 3 above, they unite to form a complete sentence.

Relatedly, if you have a grouping of words that forms an incomplete thought, is missing a verb, or is missing a subject, you have a **sentence fragment**. For example, "Parties with my friends," is a sentence fragment. Most obviously, it is missing a verb and is not a complete thought. It raises too many questions. It cannot stand alone as an independent clause, and it cannot stand alone as a complete sentence. Let's define these terms simply.

A **subject** is what is being or doing the verb. ("*I* often go...")

A **verb** is a state of being experienced by the subject or action done by the subject. ("I often *go*...")

An **independent clause** is a complete thought that contains, at the very least, a subject and a verb. It can stand alone as a complete sentence.

A **run-on sentence** joins two independent clauses incorrectly, causing sentence boundary confusion.

A **conjunction** is a linking word, such as *and, but,* or *or,* that can be used to join two clauses.

A **dependent clause** has a subject and a verb, but it is an incomplete thought and therefore cannot stand alone. Consider the independent clause, "I often go to parties with my friends." If it had a word like *while* at its start, it would become dependent on more information to make it complete: "While I often go to parties with my friends." That clause no longer stands alone; it is dependent.

A **sentence fragment** is when a dependent clause or any other kind of incomplete thought is incorrectly treated as if it were complete. A sentence fragment is never a complete sentence.

Another term you need to know is **prepositional phrase**, since prepositional phrases can get in the way of you identifying subjects and verbs. A prepositional phrase contains a preposition that often shows where something is or when it is.

Identifying Subjects and Verbs

Circle the subjects and underline the verbs in the sentences below and write down why you selected your answers:

1. In life we often set personal boundaries.

2. Sentences have boundaries too.

3. Some students think that the first sentence is correct because the topic stays the same throughout the sentence.

4. The first sentence is a run-on sentence.

5. It is missing the appropriate punctuation.

6. The verb is sometimes the action in the sentence.

7. I want to get better at correcting errors.

8. I love grammar.

9. On Tuesdays, I go to the learning lab.

10. I left my paper on my bed.

The Implied *You*

One common area of confusion that students often struggle with relates to the "implied you."

Often when there is a command, the subject, *you*, is implied rather than explicitly written down.

For example, one might say, "Sit down." This is a complete sentence because the "you" being spoken to is clearly implied and therefore, for all intents and purposes, present in the sentence.

Look at the "implied you" sentences below and identify the verb.

1. Sit down.

2. Stand up.

3. Go for a walk.

4. Know that I love you.

5. Sing loudly.

Correcting Sentence Fragments

Now that you know what a complete thought, verb, and subject are, you can correct the sentence fragments below. Remember that the minimum one needs for a complete sentence is a subject (clearly implied or explicitly stated), a verb, and a complete thought. These sentence fragments lack a complete thought, a subject, a verb, or a combination of these.

Correct each sentence fragment below. Explain why you corrected it as you did.

1. The minimum one needs.
2. Now that you know.
3. Correcting sentence fragments.
4. Susan.
5. Which is why it's important to proofread your papers.
6. The reason why I struggle with grammar.
7. Because I often procrastinate.
8. Into the paper.

Your Sentences

Write down ten sentences from a recent paper you wrote. Identify the subjects, verbs, and complete thoughts in your sentences. Next, note if any of the sentences are run-ons or fragments. It's fine if they are perfectly correct sentences! This is just an opportunity to look at your sentences in isolation from the rest of your paper. Why do you think it might be a good idea to look at your sentences in isolation from the rest of your paper?

Run-Ons and Fragments in Context

Look at the paragraph below, and highlight all run-ons and fragments. Then rewrite the paragraph correctly.

Kimberly, a student at Community College of Philadelphia, was brilliant. But she wasn't very good at identifying run-ons and fragments. It seemed to her that her sentences were fine because they made sense when she read the whole paper, no one really taught her grammar rules either. Which made her really frustrated. One day Kimberly went to the learning lab and learned the rules for correcting sentences. And fragments. She was overjoyed. On her next paper, the still had a lot of run-on and fragment errors but not as many. Be like Kimberly! When you struggle with your writing, don't be afraid to ask for help. Even if you usually don't need it.

Run-Ons and Fragments in the Real World

Go outside your classroom, dorm room, break room, or wherever you are right now, and look at the kinds of sentences you see on signs, buildings, fliers, and the like. Note three run-on sentences you find in the world. Then note three sentence fragments. Now write each incorrect run-on sentence and sentence fragment.

Beneath each, please correct the sentence so that it is a complete sentence with appropriate boundaries. Sometimes these errors are intentional, as in a paper that says *For Sale* as a title, and sometimes they are not intentional, as in *Call me, I have a great Math 116 textbook for only $60.*

Pronouns

Pronouns like *I, you, he, she, it, we, they, this,* or *that* are wonderful because they mean we do not have to keep saying the noun over and over and over again. Pronouns help us avoid situations like this:

Students often have to stand in line at financial aid. Students may not want to do this because they have to attend to their studies. Students sometimes do not have a choice.

In these sentences, using the word *they* for students would help create some variety.

Sometimes, if there are multiple nouns in a sentence or the opposite—no clear noun that the pronoun is referring to—you can confuse your reader.

Look at the examples below, then complete the activity.

Students often have to go to the financial aid window where the financial aid officers are in charge of answering questions. They can get frustrated.

The pronoun that is challenging here is *they*. Does *they* refer to the financial aid officers or the students? It may be that both are true, but as a writer you have to make clear what you mean. Here are two options for correcting the sentence above:

Students often have to go to the financial aid window where the financial aid officers are in charge of answering questions. Students can get frustrated.

or

Students often have to go to the financial aid window where the financial aid officers are in charge of answering questions. Both students and financial aid officers can get frustrated.

Another problem that often arises in papers is the nebulous (unclear) use of *this* or *that*. Imagine that you have just discussed various philosophers' points about ethics. You end your paragraph with:

This shows that there is no precise definition for ethics.

Do you mean the varying ideas of all the philosophers you spoke about in the paragraph? The ideas of the last philosopher you talked about? Your ideas? In this instance, you need to substitute *this* for a clear noun or group of nouns so your reader knows what you are referring to.

Look at the sentences below. Circle or highlight the confusing pronoun or pronouns and then rewrite the sentence with a more specific noun or nouns.

EXAMPLE:

➤ Original sentence: Reports give your readers information about various topics. They may or may not be familiar to your reader.

Rewritten sentence: <u>Reports give your readers information about various topics. The topics may or may not be familiar to your reader.</u>

1. There are different types of love according to the ancient philosophers. This is true today.

2. Revisions are important because they help you to communicate your ideas. They can often be unclear at first.

3. Lin-Manuel Miranda wrote *Hamilton* after reading a book about Alexander Hamilton. To many, he is considered a genius.

4. Oftentimes, people think of success as being a matter of luck, but it is really about hard work. That is the problem.

5. Professors could do a better job meeting the evolving needs of students. They often forget how emotionally overwhelming college can be.

6. Dan doesn't really like his pet turtle. He makes a lot of noise at night.

7. Students often want to do well, but they don't know the steps to take for writing essays. These can be daunting.

8. You might focus your binoculars on a whale in the distance or you may be interested in pointing your binoculars toward a boat party to spy on it! It is different in each of these instances.

9. It may feel helpful when someone tells you the answers to grammar questions or math problems, but they don't always stick unless you learn how to find them on your own.

10. They often write essays in the first person. It is a good strategy for writing narrative essays, but they sometimes have a hard time transitioning to more objective writing for reports.

Pronouns in Your Work

Find an essay or short piece of writing that you have completed. Write down two consecutive sentences that have pronouns in them or one sentence that has a noun followed by another sentence with a pronoun. Identify the nouns/pronouns and tell why your pronoun references are clear or whether you should revise them. Please note that you do not need to find sentences with errors for this activity. The act of identifying pronouns in two consecutive sentences in your work will help to prime your brain to check for pronoun references the next time you write.

12

Writing Clear Sentences in a Thoughtful Style

Sentence Combination

The way sentences are constructed dictates how readers engage with our work. More complex sentences challenge the reader's mind. Shorter sentences can give them a short break to process information. Sentences constructed entirely in the same way can be overwhelming to your readers and make them put down your essay. Therefore, it's good to practice the skill of sentence combination so that you are able to create sentence variety in your papers.

Look at the same example from the pronoun section on page 78:

Students often have to go to the financial aid window where the financial aid officers are in charge of answering questions. Students can get frustrated.

These two sentences can be combined into a smoother sentence in a variety of ways. Here are some options:

Students often have to go to the financial aid window where the financial aid officers are in charge of answering questions, and students can get frustrated.

This option simply uses the conjunction *and* to add information to the sentence. It emphasizes the word *students* by repeating it. The sentence gives the reader a sense that students are the most important preoccupation of the reader and perhaps subtly implies the severity of the financial aid officers' impact on students.

Students can get frustrated when they have to go to the financial aid window where financial aid officers are supposed to answer their questions.

This option places the frustration first and shifts the sentence slightly to be about how the officers are supposed to answer questions but likely don't. The emphasis in this sentence is less on the students and more on the challenges that the financial aid officers pose to students.

Financial aid workers, the people in charge of answering student questions, can often frustrate students.

This option puts financial aid workers as the subject and focuses mainly on how their actions frustrate students.

The distinctions are very subtle, but as a writer, you have complete control over how you want your thoughts to be perceived. All of these options are valid, and they will add texture to your paper. They will also help you to shape your emphasis at any given moment. Think about the various methods for sentence combination and complete the activity below.

Activity

Write down what you believe is the most effective combination of each pair of sentences below:

1. The student wanted to do a good job. He was only a freshman and didn't have the same skills as his peers.

2. Sometimes, the scholars disagree on definitions of terms. The way you define something can change your perception of it.

3. Lin-Manuel Miranda liked hip hop as a child. Lin-Manuel Miranda's father was a political consultant.

4. A research report is an objective essay that presents information on a topic that you have investigated. It is not a personal essay.

5. An infographic is a report that includes visual elements. For example, you might include graphics of cigarettes if you are creating an infographic about smoking on campus.

6. Explanations give information to answer how, why, or what questions. They do not simply present information.

7. A causal analysis speculates potential reasons for a problem or phenomenon. A causal analysis also uses research to back up the speculations.

8. One point of an argument is to help people to think in new ways about topics. Another point is also to create solutions to issues in the world.

9. A proposal provides your readers with one or more solutions to a problem. It can also provide ideas for how to handle a situation or suggestions for the allocation of funds.

10. Below is a list of steps for creating an exploratory essay. Each activity is intended to get you thinking about what to do for each step.

Sentence Combination in Your Work

Activity

Write down three pairs of sentences from a recent essay you have written. Practice combining the sentences after you write down the originals.

Subject/Verb Agreement

In English, subjects and verbs have to agree in number. In other words, you should not have a singular subject like *he* paired with a plural verb like *know*. In order to understand this concept, please read the following and then complete the activity.

We have the following pronouns or words that stand in for nouns:

Singular (one)

I

You

He/ She/They/ It

Plural (more than one)

We

They

Infinitives

An infinitive is the pure form of the verb. In English, an infinitive always has the word "to" before it. "To swim" is the infinitive and "I swim" is first person singular. The infinitive "to be" is not used in academic written English as a conjugation. Example: *You are happy* instead of *You to be happy.*

Third Person Singular

In academic written English, remember to include an "s" in the third person singular construction.

EXAMPLES:

➤ She walk to the store.

She walks to the store. [academic written English]

Mary to know the answer.

Mary knows the answer. [academic written English]

There she go.

There she goes. [academic written English]

Conjugations

If you are ever unsure of how to make a subject and verb agree, look up the following in a search engine: "English conjugation of the infinitive ＿＿＿＿＿＿＿＿."
Example: "English conjugation of the infinitive to go." In addition to any verb conjugations you may have trouble with, please memorize the following:

To Be (present tense → happening now)

I am
You are
He/ She/ It is
They are
We are

To Be (past tense → happened then)

I was
You were
He/ She/ It was
They were
We were

To Have (present tense → happening now)

I have
You have
He/ She/ It has
They have
We have

To Have (past tense → happened then)

I had
You had
He/ She/ It had
They had
We had

To Go (present tense → happening now)

I go
You go

He/ She/ It goes

They go

We go

To Go (past tense → happened then)

I went

You went

He/ She/ It went

They went

We went

Activity

Now correct the subject/verb errors in the sentences below. All of the sentences should remain in the present tense. The present tense tells what is happening now.

1. She go to the store.

2. The dog walk every day.

3. They reads many books.

4. The weather be intense.

5. The student learn very easily.

6. We knows the answer.

7. The stars, in the sky, is visible.

8. The snowflake fall on my nose.

9. You asks too many questions.

10. One way to be happy are by reading.

Vocabulary Development in Papers

There are many ways to improve your vocabulary, and the strategy that many college students choose is to look up synonyms (words that mean the same thing) in a thesaurus. The problem with this method is that, oftentimes, the words don't mean exactly the same thing. If you have never used the word before, you will be missing subtle denotations and connotations of the words. In other words, the new potentially "bigger" word you choose will be communicating something different from what you'd like to communicate. First, answer the following questions about this paragraph and your vocabulary development process. Then, complete the activity.

1. What is *denotation*?

2. What is *connotation*?

3. When you want to increase your vocabulary in general, what do you personally do and why?

4. When you want to improve your vocabulary in your papers, what do you do and why?

Activity

One way to try out new words that works really well is using words you have seen or heard before. You are likely reading books or articles that have *new* words in them. By *new*, I do not necessarily mean words you've never *seen* before, but I do mean words you have never *used* before. Go back into one or more books or articles that you have read for this class and find some vocabulary words you personally have not used from these sources. List them below. After the word, write, in quotation marks, the sentence where it appeared in the book or article. Write the dictionary definition of the word that is closest to the meaning in the sentence where it appears. Then write your own sentence with the word.

Activity

Try to incorporate two of the words above into your next paper. In order to do that, write your topic and then brainstorm possible sentences that might contain the vocabulary word. For example, let's say the topic of your next paper is homelessness and one of your vocabulary words is *obfuscate*. You might write the following sample sentence:

Sometimes existing resources for homeless people obfuscate the problems that still exist for homeless populations.

Notice that the practice sentence contains the word "homeless," which is part of your theme. It also contains your vocabulary word. You don't need to force the exact sentences you write into your paper, but it's helpful to think about possible sentences before you begin to write the next paper. That way, your brain is primed to try to use a few new words.

Once you've completed the activity, ask yourself: Did this process work for you? If so, why? If not, what other techniques might you try?

Specificity and Precision of Language

Sometimes people feel that specificity and precision of language is reserved for personal and narrative essays or other forms of creative writing. You can certainly hone your precision skills through practicing these forms of writing, and in fact, the first activity below is going to ask you to do just that! However, specificity and precision of language is important for every type of essay you write. Even if you are writing a research report, the language you use and the specificity of your details can make a difference between an A paper and a C paper. It can make a difference in your readers understanding what you are saying or putting your paper down.

The stakes can be higher than you think! The activities below are intended to help you develop precision in your language.

Has a teacher ever written "be specific" in the margins of your paper? If so, how did you react? Do you think you are good at using specific, precise words in your paper or is this something you need to work on? Explain why or why not.

Activity

The haiku is a form of creative writing that was developed in Japan. It is a poetic form that often has a prescribed set of syllables or voiced vowel sounds in each line. Haiku are short sensory glimpses into the world. One of the main reasons why writing a couple of haiku can help you with attention to language and precision is that they are very short. Unlike your papers, which are pages long, many haiku follow the pattern of five syllables (line 1), seven syllables (line 2), and then five syllables (line 3). Contemporary haiku do not always follow that exact pattern. Look at the sample haiku below by contemporary haiku poet Barry George, which has a different syllabic pattern but the same three lines and a more traditional second line. After reading Barry George's poems, complete the activities.

> after the storm
> he is rich in umbrellas —
> the homeless man
>
> off to school
> a father and two
> little umbrellas
> *Credit: Barry George*

1. What image or object appears in both poems? How does it appear differently in both poems?
2. Which of the five senses do these poems most appeal to? How do you know?

Activity

1. What is an object that is near you right now that is interesting to you or one about which you have a strong opinion? For example, does your mechanical pencil keep breaking? Is someone's bright red sweater still hanging on the hook in the back of the room? Write that object here.
2. Write one or more haiku about that object. Be as specific as possible.
3. Now take any three lines of a recent essay and turn them into a haiku using the traditional syllabic pattern.
4. Look at your haiku. What do you need to add to make it more interesting? What might you need to take away?
5. Revise your haiku.

Description and Paragraph Expansion

In order to describe objects, moments, or ideas, it is a good idea to use specific language. The activity below is designed to get you thinking about how to describe specifically and how to expand your paragraphs without just "padding" them for the sake of hitting page quotas.

To describe, think of the senses (touch, taste, smell, sight, hearing). Instead of saying *the bucket*, say *the blue bucket with the smooth handle that I found on my fourth birthday*.

To expand paragraphs, ask yourself "who," "what," "where," "when," and "why" questions. For example, if you described a reason for a political policy, you might then talk about who was involved.

Activity

Select a photograph that speaks to you. Then write a paragraph that is as specific as possible that is about or inspired by that photograph.

Highlight two sentences that could be made more sensory and one sentence that could be expanded to answer "who," "what," "where," "when," "why," and "how" questions. Then rewrite the paragraph. Make sure it is more sensory and expanded.

Activity

Take a look at the sentences below and turn them into sentences that are more specific, following the example below.

Original Sentence: There are many homeless people in Philadelphia.

Revision A: Amid the hustle and bustle of shoppers on 17th and Walnut Street in Philadelphia, you will find corners speckled with homeless veterans asking for money.

Revision B: According to Project Home, there were 15,000 Philadelphians who used shelters in 2015 (Facts on Homelessness).

Note that the way you revise your sentences depends on the type of paper that you are writing. Sometimes you have to add precision through your language choices. As was true in your haiku, the first revision makes the sentence much more sensory and engaging. The second revision, appropriate for forms of writing like reports, explanations, and evaluations, adds specific information, in this case data about the use of shelters in Philadelphia.

1. **Original Sentence:** I walk home from school late at night.
2. **Original Sentence:** This college has a lot of extracurricular programs.
3. **Original Sentence:** In 2018 President Trump made a policy that impacted many people.
4. **Original Sentence:** The dollhouse was disturbing.
5. **Original Sentence:** The president of the college has more to do with student success or failure than you would think.

6. **Original Sentence:** *Wicked* is a good musical.

7. **Original Sentence:** The impact of the arts is widespread.

8. **Original Sentence:** The ladybug walked on my paper, and I had an idea.

9. **Original Sentence:** I learned to read because my mom made me.

10. **Original Sentence:** The best way to grow is to be open to changing your perspective.

Activity

Select a paper that you have written recently, and write down at least five sentences that you might be able to revise. First write the type of paper it is and the conventions of that paper. In other words, can you revise your sentences using subjective information (opinion based) or do you need to stick to the facts? Is there room for more creative and/or sensory sentences in this paper? After you have answered these questions, work on revising some of your sentences. Please note that you may want to steer away from the topic sentences (the first sentences of each paragraph) as they can often be intentionally general.

Transitions

Transitions help your reader get smoothly from one sentence to the other or one part of an essay to another. Sometimes you can use transition words to achieve this movement. Sometimes it is best to form a bridge between sentences instead of repeating the language in one sentence in the next sentence.

Activity

Draw a literal bridge between the two figures below.

Here are two sentences about the picture above. Circle the sentence pairing that contains the most helpful transition.

1. *There were two stick figures on the page. They were basically the same.*

2. *The two siblings were mostly the same. However, one had a hairstyle that made the other jealous.*

   The second sentence contains a helpful transition. You might also form a bridge transition between the two sentences like this:

3. *The two siblings were basically the same. Their similarity ended with hairstyle.*

   Note that the repetition of the same/their similarity helps to link the two sentences together.

Activity

Below is a list of selected transition words. Look at the list and then complete the activity by adding a transition word or creating a bridge transition between the two sentences.

To Add Information: In addition, Additionally, In the same way

To Show Contrast: However, In contrast, Even though

Examples: In other words, That is to say, For example

Space: In the center, To the left, To the right

Time: First, Second, Third, Later, Formerly

Now create a transition between each of the sentences below:

1. **Original Sentences:** Sometimes violence can be invisible. There are many women and men who suffer from emotional abuse.

2. **Original Sentences:** In our society, children sometimes can't get enough to eat. They can't get enough emotional support.

3. **Original Sentences:** Going to watch a dancing show can provide great emotional relief to you, especially if you are a busy college student. It's not the best idea on the night before a paper you haven't started is due.

4. **Original Sentences:** The first step to write a successful essay is to decide you want to write it. Get out your computer.

5. **Original Sentences:** The photograph by Cindy Sherman contains a long-faced clown in the center of the composition. There are rainbow colors.

6. **Original Sentences:** There were two orange tabbies. They were basically the same.

Activity

Find pairs of sentences in a paper you have recently written. Create new transitions between each of the sentences. Please note that you may have perfectly excellent transitions between your sentences already, but experimenting with different transitions can really help you to practice different transition strategies that are available to you.

Research Skills

Paraphrasing

People tend to find paraphrasing challenging because it forces you to understand sentences on a very deep level. If you do not understand a sentence fully, you will not be able to paraphrase it accurately. Do not be intimidated! Paraphrasing can be mastered with practice.

Paraphrasing is putting a short amount of text in your own words while still giving proper credit to the author in the form of a citation. There are many ways to do this including looking at a sentence, looking away from the sentence, and magically putting it in your own words! Some people, especially those who have a lot of experience with reading and/or research, do not have to go through individual steps for this process. However, these steps can be very helpful if you are struggling with paraphrasing or if you want to get better at paraphrasing.

Paraphrasing Steps

1. Read the sentence(s) and understand it/them in the context of the article. Then write the sentence down with quotation marks.

2. Do a vocabulary annotation on the sentence (write down the vocabulary words and their definitions).

3. Put the sentence in your own words in your head or out loud to a friend.

4. Change the syntax (order) of your reworded sentence and make sure it still makes sense.

5. Your sentence should be about the same length as the original.

6. Create citation (author, page number).

EXAMPLE:

➤ *Quotation:* "Community College of Philadelphia should have better athletic equipment," according to Jeb Jones, a student at the college who wrote about the issue in an essay entitled "CCP Needs Work" (4).

➤ *Paraphrase:* According to Jeb Jones, in an essay called "CCP Needs Work," there could be much improvement in the paraphernalia for sports at the Community College (4).

What is different about the paraphrased example? Why is there a number four in parentheses?

Activity

1. Select an article that you have read this semester and write down the title and the author.

2. Select a quotation from the article that is at least two consecutive sentences. After the quotation, write the page number following the model above. Then do a vocabulary annotation on the quotation.

3. Paraphrase, starting with the second sentence and moving to the first. Add a citation to your paraphrase.

4. Read your paraphrase. Does it make sense on its own? Does it mean the same as the original? If not rewrite it, remembering to still include the citation.

Quotation Sandwich

Have you ever gone to a fast-food restaurant and been given a burger with a bun missing? Hopefully not! What would it be like if you went to a restaurant expecting a full burger and just being handed the meat from the center? First, it might get on your hands and make your hands sticky. It would be hard to eat and probably not taste so good. You would probably ask for your money back. When you are incorporating a quotation into an essay, you also want to make sure that you don't just provide your readers with the meat of your paragraph (the quotation). You have to give the readers something to hold onto to understand your quotation. Below is a method for incorporating quotations into paragraphs.

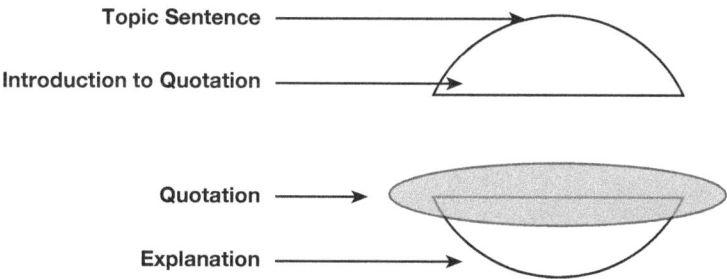

Quotation: "Community College of Philadelphia should have better athletic equipment, like badminton rackets that don't break, and fully inflated basketballs" (Jones 4).

Paragraph Incorporating Quotation

One of the ways that Community College of Philadelphia could be improved is to improve various aspects of its athletic program. There are often articles written in the school newspaper about this topic. A recent article by Jeb Jones stated, "Community College of Philadelphia should have better athletic equipment like badminton rackets that don't break and fully inflated basketballs" (4). I agree with Jones that the school should purchase better athletic equipment. The other day, I went to the athletic center and a badminton racket broke while I was playing. One way that the school could get money for better equipment would be to have a raffle after graduation.

Activity

1. Highlight each of the hamburger labels in a different color and then highlight the sample paragraph with corresponding colors. For example, you could highlight the *topic sentence* next to the hamburger in pink and highlight the topic sentence of the paragraph in pink.

2. Write down a quotation with citation.

3. Practice putting that quotation in a quotation sandwich paragraph following the example above.

13

Activities for Improving Your Writing

Revision Activity

1. Write about the process of writing your last essay. What did you do first, second, third, and so on?

2. Write about any academic challenges you had writing your last essay.

3. Write about any emotional challenges you had writing your last essay (example: procrastination).

4. What do you want to make sure you do next time regarding your essay process?

5. What do you want to make sure you don't do next time regarding your essay process?

6. Based on your instructor's feedback, what are three specific skills you are going to work on before you write your next essay? For example: *I am going to reread my essay a third time to look for run-on sentences and sentence fragments. I will make sure that I add three more specific details than last time. I will write a longer conclusion.*

Peer Review Activity

First read your partner's essay. Then answer the following questions:

1. Review the possible structure for your partner's essay. Below, write down at least three sentences that follow the essay structure. Label these sentences with their names. Some examples include topic sentences, thesis statements, introduction, and so on.

2. Write down the most specific or precise moment in the essay and explain whether or not it is effective.

3. Write down a sentence where vocabulary is being used well in the essay.

4. If you feel comfortable, offer two specific critiques of your partner's writing. Please do not offer critiques in areas where you most struggle. For example, if you routinely make sentence boundary errors, focus instead in offering suggestions in essay structure (if you have had success in essay structure).

5. Discuss your answers with your partner. Then write down what you learned from reading your partner's essay.

Thesis Statement Activity

This activity can be done with fellow classmates inside or outside of the classroom. Follow the steps below to write a compelling and effective thesis statement:

1. On an index card or a piece of paper, write down the thesis statement for whatever essay you are working on, following the guidelines you were given in class or the guidelines in your textbook.

2. Get at least four people to stand at the front of the room and read your thesis statement to them.

3. If they agree with your thesis statement they should move to the right and if they disagree with it they should move to the left. If they are confused or neutral, they should stand in the middle.

4. Ask the people at the front questions about why they are standing where they are standing and take notes.

If there are a lot of people in the middle, your thesis statement may not be arguable enough. Some people may be confused by your thesis statement and also be in the middle. If everyone is agreeing, consider your audience. Is your audience people who already agree with you? Do you want this? If everyone disagrees, make a note that you have to make extra effort at convincing your audience. If the people in the front of the room give examples for their perspectives, write them down to potentially use (with attribution) or refute as needed. Feel free to switch roles after you have gotten the notes you need.

Topic Sentences Activity

Depending on the type of essay you are writing, the topic sentences can be very different. Here is an activity to help you with essays that are less analytical and contain more narrative elements.

Highlight the topic sentences and tell how you know that they are the topic sentences.

1. Here is an overview of a place that's significant to my life: Atlantic City. Atlantic City is in New Jersey. It takes two hours to get there. It has go carts and an art cave. The beach is nice and relaxing. The water is very cold; it has

shells in the water. Atlantic City is always crowded. The restaurants are good. My family and I go there every summer. We always walk the boardwalk which is very long. There are many opportunities to have fun with your family in Atlantic City!

2. My family and I have a lot of memories there. My mom gets free rooms so we always stay at the Four Seasons or Bally's hotel. One time when we were at Four Seasons, my brothers and I took a four-hour-long walk on the beach at 7 a.m. This was a great memory because usually we do not like each other, but this time we really bonded. In addition, I remember going to the all-you-can-eat buffet and trying crab legs for the first time when I was very young while in Atlantic City. I would like to continue to make memories there.

Using Models Activity

Follow the steps below to look deeply at a piece of writing that is the same as your piece of writing:

1. Write down the type of writing that you are working on here. For example, research study, argument, persuasive essay, and so on.

2. Find an essay that is in the genre you are writing. Use your writing textbook to find the article or go online to your library database. You might have a sample from your teacher, or you could use a successful sample student essay provided by your teacher. Below is a selected list of websites that you can use to find articles in the genre that you may be writing if you do not have access to these sources. Note, find these sources by going into a search engine and typing in both the genre and the source (example: feature story, *New York Times*). If the type of article you are writing is not listed below, type the genre with the word "example" into a search engine or ask your instructor or fellow classmate for ideas.

   a. Feature Story — *The New York Times* or *The Guardian* online

   b. Research Report — *Rockefeller Archive Center*

   c. Infographic — *Wired*

   d. Causal Analysis — *Science Direct*

   e. Research Study — *Psychology Today*

   f. Flow Diagram — *Google Image*

   g. Argument — *Washington Post* Op-Ed Section

3. Decide how you want to work with the article. The instructions below will ask you to highlight/copy down information, so if you have access to a printer or copy machine, that might be a good strategy. You might also write down the information for the following questions in your notebook or in a document on a computer.

4. What is the title of the piece? Does the title make clear the genre of the piece? What about the title might inspire a title for your piece or a revision of your current title?

5. Does this piece contain a thesis statement? If so, what is it and where is it located? Is the thesis statement direct or implied? Is the thesis statement or lack of thesis statement consistent with what you learned about this genre of writing?

6. Copy down or highlight the first sentence of the first three paragraphs in this essay (excluding the introductory paragraph). Do these sentences convey the overall point of the paragraphs or do they serve a different function? What can you learn from them?

7. Write down two supporting details in this essay. Do the supporting details tend to be personal examples, statistics, or quotations from other sources? All of the above? Make a comment about how these points are balanced in the article. Are all personal examples in one paragraph and all statistics in another? Is there a blend of information?

8. Write down three vocabulary words in this piece of writing. How might you use them in your writing?

9. What is contained in the conclusion of this essay? How is it structured?

10. What do you find to be successful about the content of the article (the overall points the article is making)?

11. What do you find to be successful about the structure and rhetorical strategies of the article (how it was written)? What strategies would you like to use in your paper or in a revision of your paper?